THE STATE OF
THE ENVIRONMENT
IN OECD MEMBER COUNTRIES

**ORGANISATION
FOR ECONOMIC CO-OPERATION AND DEVELOPMENT**
PARIS 1979

The Organisation for Economic Co-operation and Development (OECD) was set up under a Convention signed in Paris on 14th December 1960, which provides that the OECD shall promote policies designed:

- to achieve the highest sustainable economic growth and employment and a rising standard of living in Member countries, while maintaining financial stability, and thus to contribute to the development of the world economy;
- to contribute to sound economic expansion in Member as well as non-member countries in the process of economic development;
- to contribute to the expansion of world trade on a multilateral, non-discriminatory basis in accordance with international obligations.

The Members of OECD are Australia, Austria, Belgium, Canada, Denmark, Finland, France, the Federal Republic of Germany, Greece, Iceland, Ireland, Italy, Japan, Luxembourg, the Netherlands, New Zealand, Norway, Portugal, Spain, Sweden, Switzerland, Turkey, the United Kingdom and the United States.

**

TABLE OF CONTENTS

The following signs and abbreviations are used in Figures, Tables and Annexes:

..	:	not available
-	:	nil or negligible
.	:	decimal point
billion	:	thousand million

OECD - Europe: All European Member countries of OECD., i.e. countries in EEC plus Austria, Finland, Greece, Iceland, Norway, Portugal, Spain, Sweden, Switzerland and Turkey.

OECD - Total : All Member countries of OECD., i.e. countries of OECD - Europe plus Canada, United States, Japan, Australia and New Zealand.

PHOTOS: Cover page and p. 30: SALGADO Jr.
        p. 2: BRAGA
        p. 50: USIS
        p. 64: USIS
        p. 80: Ministry of Foreign Affairs, Japan
        p. 88: W.H.O.
        p. 98: DEJARDIN-RAPHO
        p.108: HUBERT

LIST OF FIGURES

5

LIST OF TABLES

ANNEXES

Annex 1 — Growth in the value of agricultural production, OECD countries, 1965-1975.

Annex 2 — Composition of agricultural production, as a percentage of the total, selected countries, average for 1973 and 1974.

Annex 3 — Population economically active in agriculture, total and per km2 of agricultural land, OECD countries, 1965-1975.

Annex 4 — Tractors and combined harvester-threshers in use, total and per km2 of arable and cropland, OECD countries, 1965-1975.

Annex 5 — Consumption of commercial nitrogenous, phosphate and potash fertilizers (N,P,K), total and per km2 of arable and cropland, OECD countries, 1965-1975.

Annex 6 — Consumption of commercial nitrogenous fertilizers, total and per km2 of arable and cropland, OECD countries, 1965-1975.

Annex 7 — Catches of fish, crustaceans and cephalopods, by major marine areas, 1965, 1970 and 1975.

Annex 8 — Fish production by use, OECD countries, 1976.

Annex 9 — Industrial production indices, total output and selected industries, OECD countries, 1965 and 1975.

Annex 10 — Production and assembly of motor vehicles, OECD countries, 1965, 1970 and 1975.

Annex 11 — Growth in total and urban populations, OECD countries, 1965-1975.

Annex 12 — Growth in stocks of dwellings and road networks, OECD countries, 1965-1975.

Annex 13 — Growth in stocks of passenger cars in use, total and per 1,000 inhabitants, OECD countries, 1965-1975.

Annex 14 — Growth in road passenger and goods transport, selected countries, 1965-1975.

Annex 15 — Growth in energy consumption, total and per capita, OECD countries, 1965-1975.

Annex 16 — Total annual water withdrawal, selected countries, 1975.

Annex 17 — Annual mean levels of biological oxygen demand (BOD), selected rivers, 1965-1975.

Annex 18 — Domestic waste water treatment, selected countries, 1965-1975.

Annex 19 — Annual mean concentration of Nitrates, selected rivers, 1965-1975.

Annex 20 — Land use in OECD countries, 1975.

Annex 21 — Area of Habitable Land, built-up area, OECD countries, mid-1970s.

Annex 22 — Consumption of agricultural land for built-up uses, selected countries, 1960-1970.

PREFACE

Environmental reporting is today an important activity of the governments of Member countries. It is a way of responding to public demands for environmental information, it assists in the definition, implementation and evaluation of environmental policies and it helps to incorporate environmental concerns in decision making.

The Environment Ministers of the OECD, meeting in Paris on 7th and 8th May, 1979, approved a Recommendation on Reporting on the State of the Environment. They recommended that Member countries should prepare periodic national reports on the state of the environment and generally should improve the basis for providing information on environmental matters. They also called for the preparation by the OECD of a periodic international report on the state of the environment of the OECD region.

The first of these OECD reports is presented in this book. It assesses the state of the environment at an international level. It reviews the pressures exerted by human activities on the environment and it analyses the responses of the public, public decision makers, enterprises and the international community to the challenge of how to continue reaping the benefits of economic growth while avoiding undesirable or unacceptable damage to the environment. The report assesses the state of the environment as a result of both these pressures and responses.

The report, based on an intensive review, has been undertaken as part of the programme of work of the Environment Committee and of the Group of Experts on the State of the Environment. It draws upon information in national reports on the state of the environment and in national environmental statistical yearbooks now published or under preparation in a majority of countries. It makes use as well of results of specific surveys and projects completed by the OECD Environment Directorate.

In the course of preparing the report, it was possible to assess the state of environmental statistics and to identify their shortcomings. There are in fact many gaps in information and data, even with regard to traditional areas of concern like air and water pollution, that make difficult a comprehensive assessment of changes in environmental conditions. Moreover, available data often lack harmonization as between countries, making international comparisons difficult or, at best, tentative. Also the data available are not always usable directly in policy analysis and evaluation. This should be borne in mind in reading the report.

It is therefore hoped that this first report on the state of the environment will not only contribute to an assessment of past and emerging policies but also stimulate action designed to improve environmental statistics and reporting.

This report is issued under the responsibility of the OECD Secretariat but the success of its completion depended largely upon significant efforts by many individuals in Member countries who have contributed to it personally or officially, as well as the active support through substantive input and review of the Group of Experts on the State of the Environment and of the Environment Committee.

This report and its conclusions were presented and discussed by Environment Ministers of the OECD at their meeting in Paris on 7th and 8th May, 1979.

J.W. MacNeill

RECOMMENDATION OF THE COUNCIL
ON REPORTING ON THE STATE OF THE ENVIRONMENT

This Recommendation was approved by the Environment
Committee, meeting at Ministerial level on 8th May, 1979

The Council,

Having regard to Article 5(b) of the Convention on the Organisation for Economic Co-operation and Development of 14th December,
1960;

Having taken note of the Report on the State of the Environment
in OECD Member countries;

Considering the need for better information for the public on
the state of the environment;

Considering the importance of the relationships between pressures
induced by human activities and the response of the environment in
terms of the state of natural resources and the quality of human
life;

Considering the need for a better knowledge of the state of the
environment and its changes over time, for the purpose of a better
assessment of the results of past actions and to contribute to the
development and harmonization of environmental policies;

Considering the need for information designed to integrate more
fully environmental considerations in decision-making;

Considering the work of the OECD in the field of development and
use of statistics and indicators and particularly the Social Indicators Development Programme;

On the proposal of the Environment Committee;

I. RECOMMENDS that Member countries:

1. reinforce their co-operation within the OECD with a view to
    improving environmental information and environmental
    reporting;

2. intensify efforts to improve scientific knowledge, informa-
    tion, statistics and indicators on the state of the environ-
    ment, in order to contribute to the evaluation:
    - of the state of the environment,
    - of activities that have an impact on the environment,
    - and of environmental policies themselves,

with emphasis on important areas in which comparable and practicable indicators can at the present stage be defined;

3. prepare periodic national reports on the state of the environment and its changes over time.

II. INSTRUCTS the Environment Committee:

1. to promote and facilitate the exchange of experience and information among Member countries concerning the development and use of environmental statistics and indicators, and of reports on the state of the environment in order to support Member countries' activities in this field;

2. to continue:
   - the efforts to develop comparable environmental indicators and information formats which might be used in the preparation of reports on the state of the environment,
   - and to improve methods for the assessment, on a continuing basis, of environmental changes in important areas (through techniques such as basic monitoring of pollution, remote sensing, ecological mapping, special surveys and inventories),
   in order to arrive at a core set of comparable environmental information for OECD Member countries;

3. to ensure that a periodic report on the state of the environment of OECD Member countries is prepared and issued, to the extent practicable and appropriate, on the basis of national reports on the state of the environment and of a core set of comparable environmental information, and to report to the next Meeting of the Environment Committee at Ministerial level, if such a Meeting is decided by the Council at a later stage;

4. to carry out these tasks, taking into full account, the work of other international organisations, concerning particularly environmental statistics and assessment of the state of the environment;

5. to report to the Council on the measures taken pursuant to this Recommendation.

INTRODUCTION

This is the first review of the state of the environment in OECD Member countries. It comes at an appropriate time, a time when there is a shift under way from what may be called first to second generation environmental policies. During the period roughly up to 1975, governments were concerned primarily with setting up institutions and adopting new laws and regulations to abate and control environmental pollution. Today a second generation of environmental policies is emerging. In addition to the abatement of gross pollution there is a growing commitment to the wise husbandry of all natural resources and to the improvement of the quality of life. In addition to conventional curative policies, anticipatory approaches are being adopted. These seek to ensure that growth is environmentally sound, that the side effects of environmental deterioration are prevented, that the consequences of changes in life-style are foreseen and that environmental considerations are given full weight in all major decisions. It is hoped that this review of the state of the environment will contribute to an assessment of both past and emerging policies.

Assessing the state of the environment throughout a major part of the world is not an easy task. It is, moreover, a task that cannot be treated comprehensively at this stage. There are simply too many gaps in information, statistics and scientific knowledge. In view of this, and in view of the absence of a model generally accepted by Member countries, for the assessment of interactions between human activitiy and the environment, this report presents a selective overview of developments within OECD regions.(1) It is hoped that this review of the state of the environment will help not only to meet increasing demands for better information, but also to stimulate action designed to improve environmental statistics and reporting.

Information in national reports on the state of the environment as well as on earlier work by the OECD has been drawn on for this review. Data from other national and international sources and from a special OECD survey on environmental trends has also been used.

1) The report should be seen as complemented by more detailed and evaluative reviews of countries' environmental policies, such as those carried out by the Environment Committee of OECD on Sweden or Japan.

The point of view adopted is that human demands and natural resources need to be balanced and that doing so generates challenges requiring action on the part of various groups and authorities.

The first part of this report examines the development of certain activities such as industry and transport which generate stresses on the environment. The second examines the condition of selected natural resources - water, land, air and wildlife. It also reviews chemical substances and noise as they affect the quality of life. The third deals with the responses of the public, government, international organisations and industry to this challenge and assesses their role in shaping the state of the environment. Finally, conclusions are presented about environmental trends, changing attitudes and the need for better environmental information.

Part One

THE CHALLENGE

Human Activities having Major Impacts on the Environment

The economic growth experienced by OECD countries up to the mid-1970s was associated with rapid industrial and urban development. One result of this activity was increased wealth. One other result was an array of pressures on the environment. Member countries were consequently faced with the challenge of how to continue reaping the benefits of economic growth, while avoiding undesirable or unacceptable damage to the environment.

This part describes the past growth and ongoing structural changes in OECD Member countries, with special reference to five selected human activities that are major determinants of the state of the environment:

i) Harvesting, which embraces the management and exploitation of certain renewable resources through farming, forestry and fishery;

ii) Industrial activity, which is a major contributor to wealth as well as a major consumer of energy and raw materials and a generator of waste;

iii) Settlements, the form and structure of which effectively determine the quality of life for the majority of people;

iv) Transport and in particular the use of cars and trucks, which consumes energy and space, influences decisions about location, and is a major generator of wastes;

v) Energy production and use, high levels of which are a particular characteristic of developed economies.

1. Harvesting

Agriculture

Between 1965 and 1975 farm output increased in all OECD countries (Table 1 and Annex 1), although in most of them at a rate slower than their gross domestic products (Table 8).(1) Livestock continued to be a major share of agricultural production except in Japan, Italy, Spain and Portugal (Annex 2). Farm labour declined steadily throughout OECD countries. And there was a tendency for the rates of growth of gross agricultural product to become more closely related to those of gross domestic products.

A number of developments in farming had adverse environmental implications (Figure 1). The relatively low standard of living provided by farming led to rural depopulation and the abandonment of

---

1) OECD (1977) "Review of Agricultural Policies in OECD Member Countries", Paris.

Table 1. GROWTH IN THE VALUE OF AGRICULTURAL PRODUCTION[a],
BY REGION, 1965-1975

CHANGE IN THE VALUE OF AGRICULTURAL PRODUCTION 1965 = 100	NORTH AMERICA	JAPAN	AUSTRALIA AND NEW ZEALAND	OECD EUROPE	OECD TOTAL
Food commodities	129	126	135	123	127
All commodities	123	125	123	124	123

NOTES: a) The data are based on FAO production index series constructed by applying regional weights based on 1961-1965 price relationships to the country production figures. Deductions were made for feed and seed used in the production process.

For details see Annex 1.

Figure 1

CHANGES IN MANPOWER, FARM MACHINERY
AND USE OF COMMERCIAL FERTILIZERS
per km^2 of agricultural or arable and cropland, by region, 1965-1975

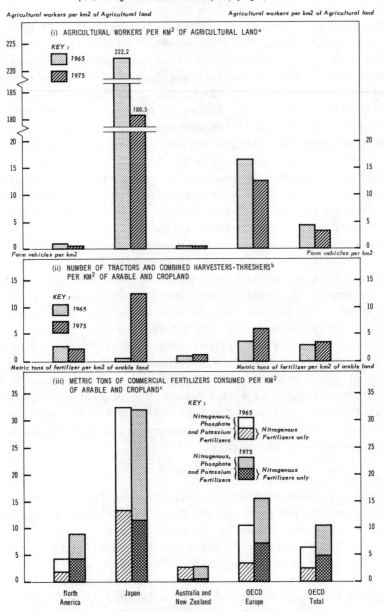

a) Agricultural land is defined as total arable, crop and permanent grassland as given in Annex 20.

b) The data refer to both wheel and crawler tractors used in agriculture and to combined harvester-threshers. The assumption that all tractors are used exclusively on arable and cropland is less satisfactory for countries where such machines play an important role in livestock rearing and forestry.

c) The data refer to nitrogenous, phosphate and potassium fertilizers. The assumption that they are used exclusively on arable and cropland is less satisfactory for countries where significant amounts of such fertilizers are applied to permanent grassland or forestland.

For details see Annexes 3, 4, 5 and 6.

farm husbandry.(1) The growth of towns and inter-city highways
that took place was often at the expense of first quality arable
land (Annex 22).

New farm practices were adopted. The dedication of entire
farms to a single crop, the enlargement of fields by uprooting hedges
to permit the use of tractors and other machines, the drainage of
wet lands and the use of pesticides affected wildlife by removing
traditional sources of food, disrupting or destroying habitats and
spreading toxic substances. Increased irrigation led to mounting
consumption of water and to the accelerated leaching out of nitrates
and other pollutants. The growing use of chemical fertilizers continued to affect the quality of water bodies. A more careful use of
chemicals was also evident prompted no doubt by rising costs, but
also perhaps by an increasing awareness of their environmental impact. In Germany, for instance, the use of potassium levelled off
while that of phosphates declined slightly.

There were also some more far reaching developments. The adoption of a "new agriculture" aimed at improving nutrition and health
while protecting the environment and conserving energy seems to be
gaining ground. Two basic thrusts may be identified in the "new
agriculture". One involves a reduction in agricultural wastes
through economic use and recycling of by-products. The other involves the adoption of new technologies such as the use of nitrogen
producing bacteria to replace nitrogenous fertilizers, and the cultivation of crops with higher efficiency in the conversion of solar
energy. The emergence of such developments reflects growing concern
not only for more efficient farming, but also for the high levels
of pollution, soil exhaustion and resource consumption associated
with high technology farming.

Forests

Forests provide habitats for wildlife, influence climate, regulate water cycles and protect land from soil erosion and desertifi-
cation. Forests also comprise the major source of ligneous raw materials for the timber, pulp, paper and allied industries and they
satisfy a large number of recreational demands.

For more than two decades wooded areas have accounted for 30 per
cent of the land area in OECD countries (Figure 11 and Table 10).
Of this only about half is considered to be suitable for regular
harvesting. Forests are vulnerable to fire, to diseases and to
predators, as well as to pollutants. Their area and sustainable
yield are affected by land clearance for farming, for road-building,
and for urban expansion. Forest resources can also be damaged by

1) OECD (1976) "Land Use Policies and Agriculture", Paris.

20

over-exploitation and by over-use for recreation. Long-term management strategies need to be applied more rigorously in the future in order to ensure that both economic and ecological objectives are achieved.

Fishing

The world harvest of fish increased from 54 million tons in 1965 to 72 million tons in 1976, with a tendency for catches to level off after 1973 (Figure 2).(1) In 1976 the OECD catch from marine waters was 42 per cent of the world tonnage. Of this total, 60 per cent was used for human consumption and 40 per cent for industrial use.(2) In 1976 OECD countries produced about half of the world's total fishmeal used primarily for animal feed (Annex 8). The tendency for catches to stabilize in recent years reflects the vulnerability of all commercially acceptable fish stocks. Some major fishing grounds (Figure 2), such as those of the North-East Atlantic, have experienced severe over-exploitation of certain species of fish.

It should be pointed out that when overfishing has destroyed or diminished fish resources, it has changed the balance between living resources of the sea. The main victim of such changes have been the fishermen who were pushed by marketing factors to destroy those very resources which were commercially more profitable. In other words, when fisheries can be the victim of pollution - and some coastal examples are well-known - they can also be the victim of their own excessive unregulated development.

The period 1965-76 marked for fishing on the high seas the end of an epoch virtually free from any restrictions. By 1977 most countries had on a "de facto" basis extended to 200 miles their sovereignty over fishing. They therefore have the means of exercising a better management on the living resources of the sea, but the efficiency of the measures taken depends in most instances on bilateral or multilateral agreements.

2. Industry

Industrial production grew between 1965 and 1975 in all OECD countries, though at different rates. It more than doubled in some countries such as Greece, Spain and Japan, while it grew much more slowly in others such as the United States and the United Kingdom (Table 2 and Annex 9).

---

1) FAO (1977) "The State of Food and Agriculture", Rome.
2) OECD (1977) "Review of Fisheries in OECD Member Countries 1976", Paris.

The general growth trend, which appears to be levelling off in most countries, is only a rough guide to the demands and pressures that are placed upon the environment. The impact of industry varies greatly from one sector to another and depends upon the structure of the economy in individual countries. It is significant that industries that consume more energy, water, wood and other resources usually generate more residuals and pollutants. Some industrial activities affect not only the working conditions of their employees, but also the quality of life of entire communities.

In general, industry has become less polluting with the development of improved production techniques, the progressive modernisation of older plants and their replacement by new, and cleaner ones. An example is provided by the pulp and paper industry(1) which is traditionally a major polluter of water. The cooking of fibres with sulphite has gradually been replaced with less polluting technologies using sulphates. In some cases water recycling has been introduced into the pulping process and has reduced the volume of effluents. In other instances oxygen bleaching is being used to render effluents less harmful. Completely new, less polluting production techniques, based on thermo-mechanical or alkaline-oxygen pulping, are also under development. Numerous examples exist, which indicate that pollution control laws and regulations have prompted industry to develop new production techniques which reduce residues previously released into the environment. Once developed, these techniques are often more widely adopted because of their practical value or demonstrated profitably.

Resource conservation is also being stimulated through new laws, regulations and programmes, as well as through public information campaigns. These efforts in industry include the identification of resource efficiency standards for products and processes; the recycling of materials such as glass and scrap metal; the recovery and re-use of products such as packaging and waste paper; and, to a more limited extent, the extension of the life of products as in the case of car tyres. Such practices also reduce pressures on the environment.

The potential hazard of certain products to health has long been recognised. This has given rise to controls, sometimes with outright bans on the manufacture, sale or use of the products. These controls have often induced product improvement or the development of substitutes.

Chemical products, such as fertilizers, pesticides, plastics, pharmaceuticals, cosmetics, dyes and other synthetic products raise particularly difficult problems. In fact, their consumption appears

_____

1) OECD (1975) "Pollution by the Pulp and Paper Industry", Paris.

Figure 2

WORLD CATCH OF FISH, CRUSTACEANS AND CEPHALOPODS[b]
by major marine areas[a], 1965, 1970 and 1975

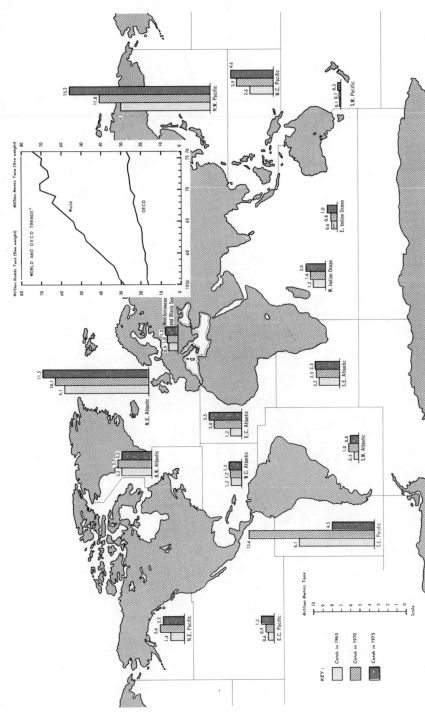

KEY:

Catch in 1965

Catch in 1970

Catch in 1975

a) The south east Pacific and north west Atlantic regions were formerly over exploited.

b) Molluscs other than cephalopods (oysters, mussels, clams, etc.) are excluded because their potential depends more on cultivation than on natural factors.

c) Figures refer to total nominal catches in marine and inland waters.

Source : OECD, FAO.

For details see Annex 7.

Table 2. GROWTH IN THE VALUE OF INDUSTRIAL PRODUCTION, TOTAL OUTPUT AND SELECTED INDUSTRIES, BY REGION, 1965-1975

CHANGE IN INDUSTRIAL PRODUCTION INDICES 1965 = 100	NORTH AMERICA	JAPAN	AUSTRALIA	OECD EUROPE	OECD TOTAL
Total industrial production[a]	130	224	139	142	142
Chemicals, rubber and petroleum and coal products	168	251	187	175	178
Motor vehicles[b]	88	362	138[c]	131	128
Iron and steel	94	258	145	117	118
Textiles, clothing and leather	102	127	115	110	108
Food, beverages and tobacco	135	150	153	141	140

NOTES:

a) The total index comprises in principle mining and quarrying, manufacturing, and electricity, gas and water.

b) Number of passenger cars produced and assembled.

c) Australia and New Zealand.

For details see Annexes 9 and 10.

25

to have doubled or trebled in most Member countries between 1963 and 1975 (Table 3). Furthermore, OECD countries account for 85 per cent of world consumption of chemicals.

While chemicals are often a boon to mankind in helping to combat ill-health and in improving the quality of life, a growing number of them appear to be hazardous. Many are toxic, others accumulate in organisms and have long-term harmful effects on health. Indeed, the past decade has been marked by a growing awareness of the range of substances that are potentially hazardous and of the complexity of their relationship to human health. Because of this situation, laws have been introduced to control the production and marketing of toxic substances, to regulate working conditions and to protect consumers. These general laws complement the more traditional selective, case by case, control of substances such as DDT, PCBs, fluorocarbons and mercury. The desirability of international effort to reduce the costs of duplicate testing of chemical products and to avoid possible impacts on international trade of different national approaches toward their control, has been reflected recently in the OECD special programme on the control of chemicals.

All signs, however, are not favourable from an environmental point of view. Modernisation of plants and processes may be slowing down due to lower rates of growth in new investments and production facilities. Also, increasing amounts of hazardous wastes have to be handled with attendant difficulties associated with safe transport, treatment and disposal.

3. Settlements

In 1965 some 680 million people, or about 21 per cent of the world total population, lived in Member countries. By 1975 this figure had reached over 750 million, or some 19 per cent of the world total. The OECD area as such thus experienced an annual population increase of between 0.5 and 1.5 per cent (Figure 3).

Population density can be viewed as a useful indicator of the stresses that human activities place upon land resources. An examination of the population density in Member countries shows that the average figure for the OECD as a whole is 23.3 persons per km^2. Nordic countries, Canada, Australia, and, to a lesser degree, New Zealand and the United States, have below average population densities, while Japan, and the majority of the remaining European Member countries are above average.

Population density related to the habitable area gives a more precise picture (Figure 13). The density of settlement is, of course, highest in urban regions and in particular where there are concentrations of population along coastlines and major valleys. Population

Table 3. PRODUCTION OF CHEMICALS AND APPARENT CONSUMPTION PER CAPITA[a], SELECTED COUNTRIES, 1963, 1970 AND 1975

PRODUCTION INDEX (1970 = 100)		COUNTRY	APPARENT CONSUMPTION (US $ PER CAPITA)		
1963	1975		1963	1970	1975
..	188	Canada	77[b]	109	285
56	123	USA	160	227	377
37	112	Japan	59	141	294
42[c]	122	Austria	56[b]	121	402[d]
52	269	Belgium[b]	70	154	334
46	136	Finland	..	130	405
50	116	France	80	141	340
48	114	Germany	130	182	424
38	158[e]	Greece	..	..	..
48	159[d]	Ireland	..	..	..
56[b]	126[b]	Italy	77[b]	115	247
35	120	Netherlands	76[b]	172	294
65	116	Norway	73	134	325
..	..	Portugal	14[b]	47	..
35	275	Spain	39	96	281
58[f]	118	Sweden	89	174	412
58[b]	111[b]	Switzerland	77[b]	155	335
63[b]	116[b]	United Kingdom .	113	165	343

NOTES:
a) Including man-made fibres.
b) Excluding man-made fibres.
c) Due to changes in measurement method, 1971 = 100.
d) 1974.
e) 1973.
f) Due to changes in measurement method, 1968 = 100.

Figure 3

GROWTH IN TOTAL AND URBAN POPULATIONS [a]
by region, 1965-1975

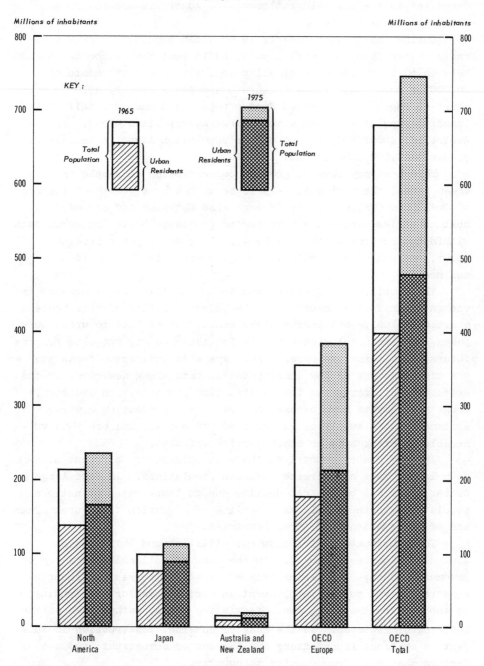

Millions of inhabitants

Millions of inhabitants

KEY :

1965

1975

Total Population

Urban Residents

Urban Residents

Total Population

North America

Japan

Australia and New Zealand

OECD Europe

OECD Total

a) OECD estimates of urban populations in settlements of 20,000 or more inhabitants (based on national contributions and national publications) unless otherwise specified. See Annex 11.

For details see Annex 11.

densities in the Rhine-Ruhr region of Germany and along Japan's Pacific coast, for example, reach over 1,400 persons/km^2. Although densities in the coastal settlements of Australia are lower, they are still significant.

During the 1960s and early 1970s urban populations grew generally faster than the total population in most Member countries and between 50 to 80 per cent of all people lived in settlements of 20,000 or more inhabitants (Figure 3 and Annex 2). By 1970, almost three-quarters of the United States population and over half of the Canadian population lived within large metropolitan areas. In Australia, about 70 per cent of the population lived in ten cities of over 100,000 inhabitants.

This tendency towards greater concentration of people in urban areas caused the period 1965-75 to be marked by a growth of the stock of dwellings (Table 4). Roads were also upgraded and extended in most countries during the same period providing better networks both within and between cities (Table 4). This development brought about, and was in turn stimulated by, changes in the location of jobs and homes.

The development of cities and their utilities has increased the use and transformation of land. The direct effects of this process are the exclusive and irreversible commitment of land to urban purposes, and the preclusion not only for the present, but also for the future, of alternative uses. There are also indirect effects such as the encouragement of low density settlements along new roads or the extraction of aggregates for construction purposes. In addition, large settlements have become increasingly dependent on complex systems for the supply of water, food and energy, and are thus vulnerable to breakdowns or other service defaults.

In many Member countries, there is evidence of a recent slowdown in the rate of increase in urban populations. In some large cities there has been a net decline due to lower rates of national population growth as well as a decline of migration from rural areas and of immigration from other countries.

The construction of transport, utilities and buildings has slowed down correspondingly. In the case of national motorway programmes, although some extensions are likely, increasing financial constraints and public involvement in decision-making are leading to emphasis on the management of existing roads, rather than on the building of new ones. In the case of housing, construction is subject to cyclical fluctuations and depends on demographic and social factors that vary from country to country.

However, some countries, such as those of Southern Europe and some specific regions such as the South-West of the United States and the South-East of France, are experiencing, for different

Table 4. GROWTH IN STOCKS OF DWELLINGS AND MOTORWAY NETWORKS, OECD COUNTRIES, 1965-1975

DWELLING STOCK (PERCENTAGE CHANGE 1965-1975)	COUNTRY	MOTORWAYS (PERCENTAGE CHANGE 1965-1975)
45	Canada	..
29[a]	USA	107
41[b]	Japan	372
36	Australia	..
29	New Zealand	69
17	Austria	95
15	Belgium	228
24	Denmark	238
21	Finland	383
23	France	430
24	Germany	84
37[a]	Greece	727
20[a]	Iceland	..
17	Ireland	..
17	Italy	218
30	Luxembourg	..
36	Netherlands	169
21[a]	Norway	650
5[a]	Portugal	–
41	Spain	1,792
23	Sweden	210
36	Switzerland	525
20[a]	Turkey	..
14	United Kingdom	258
30	North America	..
35	Australia and New Zealand	..
22	OECD Europe	190[c]
27	OECD Total	126[c]

NOTES:

a) OECD estimates made on the basis of information in national and international publications.

b) 1963-1973.

c) Based on partial totals.

SOURCE: UNO, International Road Federation.

For details see Annex 12.

reasons, significant growth in urban populations and related development activities. In several cases this is due to tourism. In
others, such as in some cities in the United Kingdom and the United
States, there is a marked movement of residents from dense, older
inner districts to homes with gardens in the suburbs. This creates
demands for building on farm land and can involve the abandonment of
old-established neighbourhoods. These developments, coupled with the
ageing of the physical stock of buildings and industrial plants in
older parts of cities, aggravate the problems of revitalisation of
inner cities.

4. Transport

The stock of cars increased in all OECD Member countries between 1965 and 1975, often at a relatively rapid rate. The stock
increased by 45 per cent in North America, 100 per cent in Europe
and nearly 700 per cent in Japan (Figure 4). Commercial vehicle
fleets also grew significantly.

The distances covered by passengers and goods increased in
nearly all countries over the same period (Table 5). Road transport
took an increasing share of all goods movements in European countries as well as in Japan.

Significant economic and social benefits accrued to OECD Member
countries from this rapid growth in vehicle use. On the other hand,
the extension of mass motoring brought increased use of land and
energy demands for transport. It also brought more air pollution from lead, carbon monoxide, unburnt fuel, nitrogen oxides and
photochemical oxidants. And it led to more congestion, noise, and
accidents that adversely affected the quality of life. Pedestrian
areas, traffic cells and other forms of traffic management helped
to alleviate some of the most acute problems. However, it is estimated that the hidden costs imposed by road users on other travellers
and upon other interests amount to some 4 per cent of the gross
domestic product of OECD countries. Even if such figures represent
only orders of magnitude, they indicate that the unaccounted costs
of vehicle use, including environmental effects, are substantial.

The first-car market is regarded as almost saturated in North
America. It is approaching saturation in most of Europe, but is
expanding rapidly in Japan, where commercial vehicles are no longer
more numerous than passenger cars. The market for second and third
cars, including recreational vehicles, is already well developed in
North America, but is only just beginning to take-off in Europe and
Japan. The stock of vehicles should become progressively less

Figure 4

GROWTH IN STOCKS OF PASSENGER CARS IN USE [a]
by region, 1965-1975

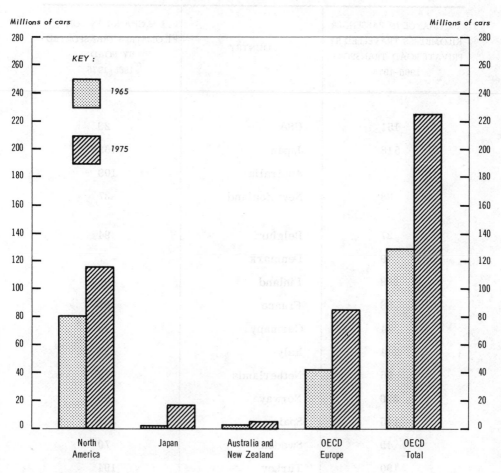

a) Millions of passenger cars in use at the end of the year.

Sources : International Road Federation (1977), "World Road Statistics 1972-1976", Washington D.C.
UNO (1976), "Statistical Yearbook 1975", New York.

For details see Annex 13.

Table 5. GROWTH IN ROAD PASSENGER AND GOODS TRANSPORT, SELECTED COUNTRIES, 1965–1975

% CHANGE IN PASSENGER KILOMETRES TRAVELLED BY PRIVATE ROAD TRANSPORT 1965-1975	COUNTRY	% CHANGE IN TON KILOMETRES TRANSPORTED BY ROAD 1965-1975
151	USA	23
518	Japan	168
..	Australia	109
88	New Zealand	37
27	Belgium	94
19	Denmark	– 7
148	Finland	96
98	France	92
74	Germany	49
244	Italy	37
95	Netherlands	72
276	Norway	65
175	Spain	311
49	Sweden	70
190	Turkey	194
53	United Kingdom	28

SOURCES: International Road Federation (1977), "World Road Statistics 1972-1976", Washington D.C.

Bureau Permanent International des Constructeurs d'Automobiles (1977), "Le rôle de l'Automobile dans l'Economie Industrielle Moderne", Paris.

For details see Annex 14.

polluting as a result of the replacement of older cars by new ones which comply with more stringent emission standards. However, this observation must be qualified. The rate of replacement of the vehicle stock is about ten years. Pollution control devices deteriorate with use and lack of proper maintenance. Thus the benefits of stock replacement are not as large as may be expected. The control of emissions from commercial vehicles is only beginning. Vehicles are becoming progressively more energy efficient, particularly in those countries presently using heavy cars. This change, however, may result in an increase in noise.

Increases in the use of cars are likely to continue. This conclusion is predicated upon expected increases in household expenditures for transport in Japan and Europe where they already reach 4 per cent and 7 to 8 per cent respectively of total consumption expenditures, as compared with 11 to 12 per cent in the United States and Canada. It is also predicated on the continuing spread of settlements, which leads to longer trips between homes, jobs and other destinations. The development of life styles, involving more time for mobility-based activities, such as tourism, should also contribute to an increase in the use of motor cars. The growth in the transport of goods by road vehicles depends not only on general economic activity but also on the competitive conditions of road transport vis-à-vis alternative modes of transport.

The scale of any adverse effects of motor vehicles on the environment depends on the size of the transport fleets. The characteristics of the technology and on the distances travelled. Major technological efforts have been made in OECD countries over the past decade to reduce air pollution and to economise in energy consumption. Thus less scope remains in the future to reduce total environmental damage and energy consumption by means of such technological developments. Continuing stresses on the environment will require that attention be focused not only on improving the vehicles themselves, but also on ensuring that vehicles are used in a manner compatible with environmental and energy conservation goals.

5. Energy

Between 1960 and the end of 1973, the total energy requirements of all OECD countries increased at an average annual rate of 5.1 per cent (Figure 5), an increase similar to that of gross domestic product. While the use of all fuels, except for coal, increased, oil consumption grew particularly rapidly, filling the gap between domestic energy demand and available indigenous supplies. The fourfold increase in the world price of oil in 1973 caused a major shift

Figure 5

GROWTH IN TOTAL ENERGY CONSUMPTION [a]
by region, 1965-1975

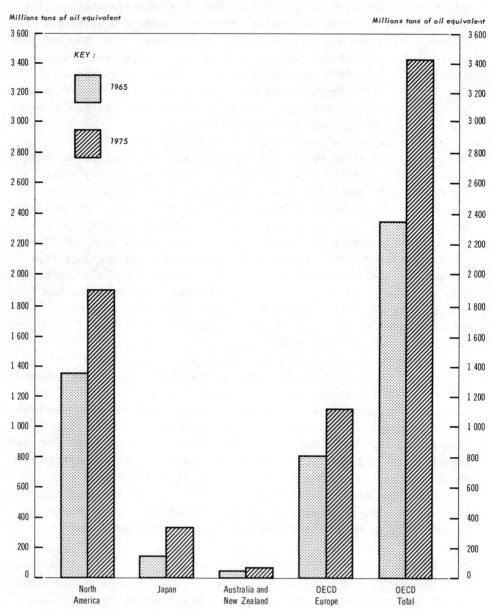

Millions tons of oil equivalent

KEY :

1965

1975

North America — Japan — Australia and New Zealand — OECD Europe — OECD Total

a) Millions tons of oil equivalent.

For details see Annex 15.

in energy supply and demand. Overall energy use actually declined
in 1974. In 1975, it began to grow again, though at a relatively
slower rate than previously.

The changes in the world oil market forced most countries to
attempt to reduce oil imports, or at least to slow down the rate of
earlier increases. Actions have been of two kinds: energy conservation, and the development of indigenous energy supplies, including
substitutes for oil. If successful these actions will inevitably
affect the overall level, the structure and the geographical
distribution of energy production and consumption and thus will also
change the impact of energy production and use on the environment.

The International Energy Agency forecasts that energy demand in
its Member countries will continue to increase although more slowly
than gross domestic product.(1) This reflects expectations of reduced rates of economic expansion, more efficient energy use, and
changing consumer behaviour. While increased energy production and
use will place greater stress upon the environment, the ability to
sustain economic growth with less energy per unit of domestic product should prove beneficial to the environment.

Significant opportunities exist to conserve energy in the domestic, commercial and industrial sectors of the economy. Several
countries have modified building codes in order to improve the
thermal efficiency of both residential and commercial buildings.
Others have introduced incentives to insulate old buildings. Dis-
trict heating, utilising waste heat from the generation of electricity, is in use in some North European countries.(2) There is
potential to increase the fuel efficiency of motor vehicles, particularly in North America where heavy cars are still in vogue.
Improved public transport, economies in the use of vehicles and more
efficient town planning may also contribute to energy conservation.
Industry, which accounts for the largest share of energy use in most
OECD countries, and which has achieved significant advances in energy
conservation in response to market forces, seems to have further
scope for significant savings.

Price changes have generated major efforts to develop offshore
oil and gas, coal, nuclear power and other energy sources as re-
placements for imported oil (Tables 6 and 7). The environmental
effect of these efforts will depend heavily upon the relative impact
of the alternative sources and on their share of total
consumption.(3)

1) IEA (1978) "Energy Policies and Programmes of IEA Countries",
   Paris.
2) OECD (1977) "Environment and Energy Use in Urban Areas", Paris.
   OECD (1978) "Heat Production and Distribution", Paris.
3) OECD (1977) "Energy Production and the Environment", Paris.

Table 6.   TOTAL ENERGY CONSUMPTION BY SOURCE, OECD, 1974-1985

ENERGY CONSUMPTION	INDEX (1974 = 100)			AS A % TOTAL CONSUMPTION[b]		
	1974	1980[c]	1985[c]	1974	1980[c]	1985[c]
Solid fuel	100	113	135	19. 8	18. 5	18. 1
Oil[a]						
Domestic	100	128	140	18.3	19.3	17.4
Net import	100	118	138	36.5	35.6	34.4
Total (less marine bunkers)	100	123	141	51. 4	52. 2	49. 3
Gas	100	107	126	20. 3	17. 9	17. 4
Nuclear power	100	373	801	1. 7	5. 1	9. 1
Hydro/Geo	100	111	128	6. 8	6. 3	6. 0
Total	100	121	147	100. 0	100. 0	100. 0

NOTES:

a)   Oil includes oil derived from natural gas processing (i.e. natural gas liquids).

b)   Wherever the columns do not sum to 100%, the differences are due to stock changes and minor contributions of other energy sources (such as solar, wind...

c)   Estimates by OECD.

Table 7.   TOTAL ENERGY INPUTS FOR ELECTRICAL POWER GENERATION, OECD, 1974-1985

ENERGY INPUTS	INDEX (1974 = 100)			AS A % OF TOTAL INPUTS		
	1974	1980[b]	1985[b]	1974	1980[b]	1985[b]
Solid fuel	100	118	149	36. 9	33. 5	31. 7
Oil[a]	100	115	137	21. 6	19. 2	17. 1
Gas	100	113	111	12. 8	11. 2	8. 2
Nuclear power	100	373	801	5. 6	16. 3	26. 0
Hydro/Geo	100	111	128	23. 1	19. 8	17. 0
Total inputs	100	129	173	100. 0	100. 0	100. 0
Electricity generated	100	127	171	36. 3[c]	35. 7	35. 7

NOTES:

a)   Oil includes oil derived from natural gas processing (i.e. natural gas liquids).

b)   Estimates by OECD.

c)   i.e. one ton of energy input (in oil equivalent) generates 0.363 tons of electrical power (in oil equivalent) in 1974.

Solid Fuel

Solid fuel production in OECD countries is projected to increase from 634 million tons of oil equivalent in 1974 to 923 million tons by 1985 and to be concentrated in a few countries (Table 6). The environmental effects of increased coal production and use remain uncertain, but the effects on health and safety are regarded as key issues in all countries. Subsidence and the disposal of waste are also major concerns in some areas. Coal mining has always been recognised as a hazardous occupation, while the burning of coal can generate substances that are a hazard to the health and safety of the general public. In Australia, Canada, Germany and the United States, there is concern about the future reclamation of open pit mines as well as the demands that mining places upon sometimes limited supplies of water.

Oil and Gas

The consumption of oil and natural gas liquids is projected to increase from 1,781 million tons of oil equivalent in 1974 to 2,137 million tons in 1985 (Table 6). During the same period, the domestic production of oil, primarily from the North Sea, Canada, Alaska and offshore United States, is projected to increase from 635 million tons of oil equivalent to between 887 and 1,008 million tons.

Accidental blow-outs during drilling are inevitable occurrences in oil exploration and development. Between 1960 and 1970 blow-outs occurred at one out of every 2,500 wells drilled on land and at roughly one out of every 500 drilled offshore. Oil spillage amounted to between 50,000 and 100,000 tons a year.

Oil transport by pipeline gives rise to land use, ecological and aesthetic impacts. Most oil is, however, transported by tankers and this results in regular operational losses and discharges of petroleum as well as oil spills due to tanker accidents (Table 9). Advances in low temperature technology have made it possible to transport and to store natural gas in a liquid form that occupies 1/600 of its normal volume. Over the next decade an increasing share of OECD Member countries' gas is expected to be supplied in this way. Some countries have experienced no difficulties to date in handling liquified gas, but the risk of accidents from tanker operations near populated areas has resulted in public resistance to, and delays in, the location and construction of receiving terminals in the United States.

Uranium

The use of uranium in nuclear plants is forecast to increase from 85.1 million tons of oil equivalent in 1976 to 435.7 million tons by 1985 (Tables 6 and 7). Under normal operating conditions,

nuclear power plants have less impact on their surroundings than
fossil fuel plants. Their major disadvantage, however, is that they
produce more waste heat per unit of power than conventional genera-
tors. Although routine radioactive emissions from nuclear power
plants are considered to be of no consequence, there is the possibility of major hazards from radioactive substances as a result of
accidents, including the leakage of contaminated waste water, or
sabotage. Radioactive waste management(1) and the disposal of materials with long half-lives and long-term genetic effects have been
recognised as important concerns with respect to public health and
have thus become essential factors in the development of nuclear
energy policy.

Electricity

Total fuel requirements for electrical power generation in OECD
Member countries are projected to increase from 1,028 million tons
of oil equivalent in 1974 to 1,787 million tons by 1985 (Table 7).
The electricity produced is projected to increase from 374 to 637
million tons of oil equivalent over the same period. This implies
an overall efficiency in converting fuel to electricity of 36 per
cent.(2) The share of electricity generated by nuclear power is
projected to increase from 5 per cent in 1974 to 26 per cent in
1985; coal is expected to remain the dominant fuel but its share
is estimated to decline from 37 to 32 per cent over the same period;
gas and oil are expected to decrease their share of the total from
13 and 22 per cent to 8 and 17 per cent respectively.

---

1) OECD (1977) "Objectives, Concepts and Strategies for the
   Management of Radioactive Waste".
2) Percentage of electricity generated to total primary energy
   input.

Table 8. GROWTH OF HUMAN ACTIVITIES AFFECTING THE STATE OF THE ENVIRONMENT, SELECTED INDICATORS, BY REGIONS, 1965-1975

Percentage increase 1965-1975

	North America	Japan	Australia and New Zealand	OECD Europe	OECD TOTAL
Value of agricultural production	23	25	23	24	**23**
Value of industrial production	30	124	39(c)	42	**42**
Urban population (a)	21	19	22	19	**20**
Passenger cars in use	45	684	71	100	**75**
Energy consumption	41	119	58	39	**46**
Gross Domestic Product (b)	33	125	54	45	**44**
Private Final Consumption Expenditure	42	112	57	48	**49**

(a) OECD estimates.
(b) 1970 prices and exchange rates.
(c) Australia only.
See Annexes 1, 9, 11, 13 and 15.

Part Two

ENVIRONMENTAL CONDITIONS

The State of the Media and Selected Concerns

Chapter 1

WATER

1. Uses and availability of freshwater

Water is the delicate support system for many forms of life and at the same time it is the natural resource most heavily used by man. It is used in households for domestic purposes, by farmers for irrigating land and by manufacturers in industry. It is a potential source for power generation and is also used for cooling in conventional and in nuclear power stations. Water is also used without withdrawal, for purposes of navigation, recreation and fishing. It is often used for more than one purpose, at the same time or in succession.

Estimates in 1975 for a number of OECD Member countries show that the volume of water withdrawal per head of population varies considerably. This is due primarily to differences in climate, manufacturing and farming practices, energy production and life styles (Figure 6). Historical evidence shows continued increases in the volumes withdrawn. In the case of the United States, where figures are available for a long period, withdrawals have increased tenfold since the beginning of this century. In all the countries for which figures are available withdrawals have grown significantly in recent years. Yet in certain countries, while domestic withdrawals increased markedly between 1965 and 1975, growth now seems to have slowed due to reduced rates of urban expansion and smaller growth in the use of household appliances. Furthermore there is evidence that the increasing cost of freshwater is beginning to affect industrial abstraction, except for cooling, and is leading to increased recycling sometimes in association with pollution control. Withdrawals for irrigation and cooling show no reduction, however, and seem bound to continue to contribute to further growth in demand.(1) Irrigation is a dominant water use in Mediterranean and semi-arid climates, where it is needed for agricultural production. Even in places with temperate climates, irrigation enables the yield from certain crops to be doubled in good years. The growth in demand for freshwater for

---

1) Cf. National reports on the state of the environment. National Water Yearbooks or Reports.

cooling purposes will depend on the location of new power plants and the extent to which cooling towers are used.

The availability of freshwater varies, of course, regionally and locally due to variations in climatic and geophysical conditions. Around the Mediterranean and in semi-arid regions of Australia and the American southwest, the availability of water has been, and is likely to be, a major limitation on economic development. Indeed, supplementing readily available supplies is often seen as a priority task. Substantial efforts have been made in such regions to overcome shortages by transporting water over long distances, connecting river basins and regulating water flows. However the requisite dams, canals, irrigation works and bore holes often involve profound changes to the environment.

The quality required for a given purpose has an important bearing on the availability of water. In the case of drinking water, quality remains satisfactory in many places, but some experts claim that it has deteriorated in some urban and industrial regions. Several reasons are cited for this deterioration in quality. An increasing number of industrial, commercial and even agricultural users are being supplied with water of drinking quality from municipal systems. The resulting increase in demand, when coupled with the growing needs of domestic users, has led to supplies being taken from sources often nearer to cities and lower in quality. Water from such sources has in turn had to be treated with increased quantities of chlorine or processed in other ways. Studies indicate that one consequence of these developments is that a number of micro-pollutants remain in the water even after treatment and that certain new micro-pollutants, such as organochlorine compounds are formed. It is thought that some of these organochlorine compounds have the potential to cause cancer.[1]

Certain countries such as France, Germany and Italy used to depend on underground water for up to 80 per cent of their public supplies.[2] These supplies, were traditionally of high quality. In some cases however, they have suffered depletion, microbial or chemical contamination and increased salinity due to excessive withdrawal, poor management and inadequate protection.

---

1) On the basis of preliminary findings from the programme on "The Control of Specific Water Pollutants", OECD.
2) Based on comparative data from Ministry of Agriculture, Sweden, "Water in Sweden", Stockholm, 1977.

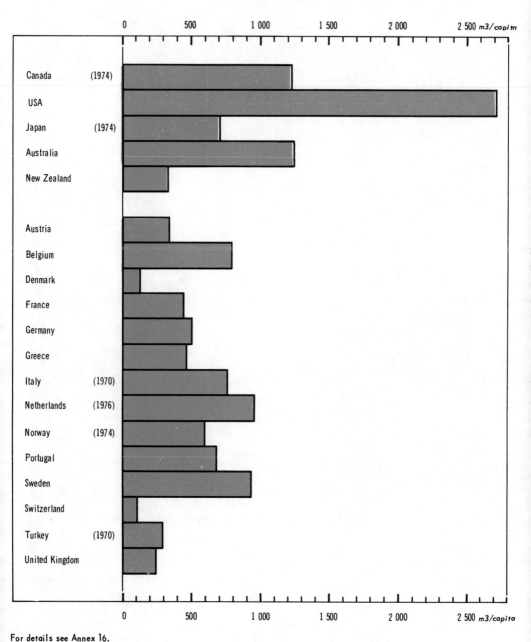

Figure 6

TOTAL ANNUAL WATER WITHDRAWAL PER CAPITA

selected countries, 1975

For details see Annex 16.

2.   Freshwater - changes in quality

General trends

Several important changes in pollution may be identified:

 i) levels of suspended solids and oxidizable matter (BOD)
    have stabilized or fallen in several Member countries; at
    the same time "micro-pollutants", pathogenic micro-
    organisms and thermal pollution are causing increasing
    concern in several countries;

ii) pollution from point sources such as urban or industrial
    outfalls is, in general, under progressively better control,
    whereas the pollution from diffuse sources, such as the
    run off from agricultural land, e.g. fertilizers, remains
    largely uncontrolled and is on the increase in most
    countries.

These trends of course, are, closely inter-connected and largely
reflect the nature and limitations of pollution control. Controls
were first introduced for emissions which could most easily, promptly
and effectively be reduced, such as those of coarse substances released from major point sources. The wide variety of micro-
pollutants originating from diffuse sources is, in general, far more
difficult to locate and control.
    A notable development has been the widespread establishment of
authorities responsible for all aspects of water resource management
for entire river basins. Specialised bodies responsible for national
water policies and for the co-ordination of the river basin authorities, have been set up at Ministerial level. Regulatory and economic instruments, such as standards and user charges, have been
systematically introduced.

Pollution by suspended solids and oxygen demanding matter
(BOD)

    Pollution by suspended solids and by matter drawing upon dissol-
ved oxygen during its decomposition has tended to level off or decline in bodies of water where action has been taken. For instance,
in the United Kingdom where rivers are classified according to their
cleanliness, the length of rivers with water in the higher quality
classes increased between 1970 and 1975. In France biological oxygen demand declined or remained stable in almost all river basins.
Concentrations of suspended solids fell in some river basins, but
increased in the most industrialised and urbanised ones between 1971
and 1975. In Japan a reduction in biological oxygen demand has been
recorded since 1971. Further evidence shows that releases of oxygen
demanding matter have also decreased or levelled off over the 1970-
1975 period in the United States, Netherlands and Sweden. Figure 7

shows that the biological oxygen demand has decreased or stabilized at the mouth of most of the major rivers considered.

These results have been achieved by means of the treatment of municipal sewage and of industrial wastes as well as by the adoption of technologies that produced less pollutants. Slower industrial growth, which led to a slower growth in the generation of pollutants was an additional reason for the decline.

The proportion of populations served by waste water treatment plants varies from less than 5 per cent to over 80 per cent in OECD countries. However the last decade has been marked by heavy investment in this field in a majority of countries (Figure 8). Unfortunately treatment plants, which are fundamental to pollution control, are in many instances not operating as efficiently as intended.[1] Explanations can be found for this in inadequate operating funds, poorly trained personnel and at times even lack of interest on the part of management. Solutions are being sought to the problems through the creation of effective financing mechanisms; the certification of personnel to ensure the development of efficient staff; and the adoption of technical means to prevent overloading or damage to treatment plants by toxic industrial effluents.

Pollution by micro-pollutants

Studies of major rivers in OECD countries have revealed the presence of several hundred detectable substances which differ widely in their characteristics. Among the substances identified are organochlorine compounds, heavy metals and organometalic compounds including organophosphorus. They find their way into the aquatic environment via domestic and industrial effluents or from diffuse sources, such as pesticides and fertilizers from agricultural areas or through atmospheric fall-out and via urban run-off. Many of these substances are persistent and they can accumulate in the food chain. Action has been taken to control some of them, such as mercury, PCBs and DDT and this has led to evidence that concentrations are in some cases beginning to fall. Multiple barrier control strategies to eliminate these pollutants have been proposed.[2] These involve intervention at the source of the pollution and strict control, either by the prohibition of the production of the chemical, as in the case of DDT, or by restricting its use mainly or solely to closed circuits, as in the case of mercury and PCBs, or by means of residuals recovery.

---

1) OECD Recommendation "Water Management Policies and Instruments", 24th April, 1978.
2) OECD Recommendation "Strategies for Specific Water Pollutant Control", 14th November, 1974.

Figure 7. ANNUAL MEAN LEVELS OF BIOLOGICAL OXYGEN DEMAND (BOD), SELECTED RIVERS, 1965-1975

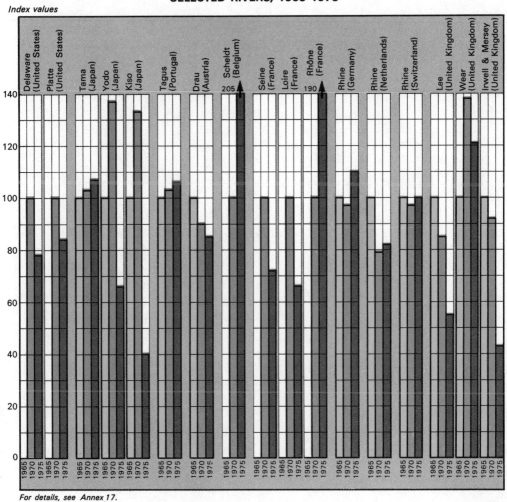

For details, see Annex 17.

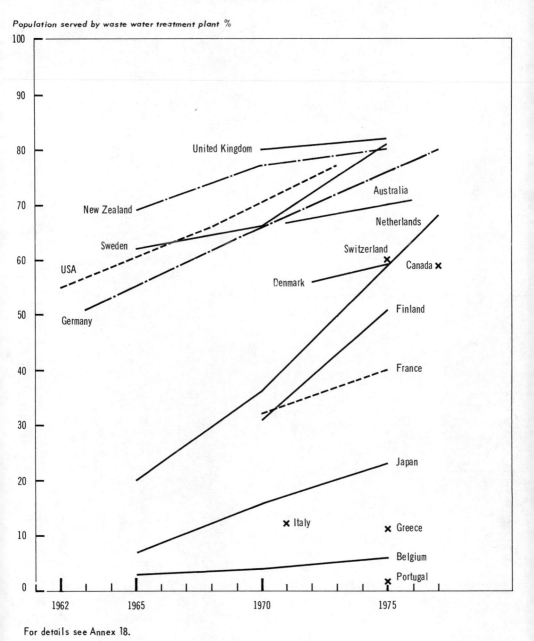

Figure 8

DOMESTIC WASTE WATER TREATMENT
selected countries, 1965 to 1975

For details see Annex 18.

Among the specific pollutants, phosphorus and nitrogen compounds, play a specific role, since they cause a particular kind of problem known as eutrophication. This phenomenon, which has increasingly affected the surface waters of OECD countries over the last twenty years, is due to the proliferation of microscopic algae stimulated by these substances. Eutrophication,[1] through the de-oxygenation of the water, leads to a deterioration in aquatic ecosystems (particularly for fish), and a degradation in acquatic ecosystems recreational areas (swimming, fishing), Furthermore, it often makes it difficult to use the water for domestic purposes even after cost-ly treatment since it adversely affects the quality of drinking water both from the point of view of taste and health.

Almost all important freshwater bodies deteriorated during the 1965-1975 period;[2] examples include the lower Great Lakes (Erie and Ontario), Alpine Lakes (like Lake Geneva). Similarly the nitrate concentration in rivers and estuaries increased almost everywhere during this period (Figure 9). The main sources responsible for eutrophication remain urban effluents and especially polyphosphates in detergents and run-off from agricultural fertili-zers that are increasingly being used (Figure 1). Understanding of the eutrophication process has advanced considerably over the last ten years. Counter measures take the form of control over phosphorus and nitrogen compounds in effluents, in detergent products and in the application of fertilizers. Although most OECD countries have taken some measures for the control of eutrophication only a few such as Finland and Sweden have enforced large-scale control.

Discharges of waste heat

Power stations take water from rivers, lakes and sea coasts, use it for cooling, and then they return it at a higher temperature. The warming of the waters that results leads the levels of dissolved oxygen to fall. This in turn affects plants and fish adversely and reduces the capability of water systems to assimilate organic com-pounds particularly in summer. Power stations can also create ther-mal barriers in estuaries that interfere with the migration of fish and with their spawning. Where the number of power stations is inc-reasing overloading of the cooling capacity of water bodies can occur.

A technologically feasible alternative is to dissipate waste heat into the air via cooling towers, but this can affect the local climate and may lead to aesthetic damage to scenery. New initiatives exist for the use of such heat in nearby homes, greenhouses and factories thereby conserving energy.

1) OECD "Scientific Fundamentals of the Eutrophication of Lakes and Flowing Waters", Paris, 1971.
2) On the basis of preliminary findings of the OECD Programme on monitoring of inland waters.

3.   Coastal waters

Coastal waters, including estuaries and continental shelves, are important for their biological activity and their socio-economic value for fishing, recreation and tourism.

During the last fifteen years or so tourist developments have expanded rapidly in many countries. Coastal sites have also been increasingly in demand for oil refineries, petrochemical plants, steel works, power plants and other forms of heavy industry. One explanation offered for the coastwards shift of heavy industry is that coastal sites constitute a loop hole in the increasingly strict apparatus for the protection of freshwater, air and land. Whatever the explanation, the result has been an increase in the pollution of marine environments. At the same time maritime countries increasingly recognise the potential vulnerability of coastal water and its value as a resource and have taken steps to manage it.(1)

Coastal waters are affected by pollution from many sources. The most common sources are industrial effluents and municipal sewage (Figure 10) which in certain estuaries cause severe de-oxygenation and interference with marine life and fisheries. Industrial wastes can introduce toxic substances that may accumulate.

Substantial increases in the monitoring of coastal and estuarine waters have taken place in recent years. Some monitoring has been done on a national basis. Some has been undertaken to satisfy international conventions, and the need to prevent transfrontier pollution has led to increased monitoring of waters receiving wastes from several countries. However, even where adequate data are available they seldom provide a long term picture of pollution.(2)

What evidence there is points to the absence of serious pollution around a large part of the marine coast of Member countries. Micro-organisms and heavy metals are however present in significant measure in some coastal areas, for example parts of the Mediterranean.(3) Where microbial pollution occurs at bathing resorts it may cause outbreaks of viral hepatitis and poliomyelitis. Shellfish contaminated by such pollution may also cause illness. In the United States pollution from sewage has led to the closing, at least temporarily, of an estimated one-fifth of the nearshore shellfish grounds. Coastal marshes, wetlands and estuaries also provide a habitat for wildlife and the contamination or destruction of these habitats has occurred due to accidental or routine discharges of pollutants or to changes in drainage.

1) OECD Recommendation on "Principles Concerning Coastal Management" adopted on 12th October, 1976.

2) UNEP "Preliminary Report on the State of Pollution of the Mediterranean Sea".

3) OECD (1975) "Mediterranean Pilot Study of Environmental Degradation and Pollution from Coastal Development", Paris.

Figure 9.   ANNUAL MEAN CONCENTRATION OF NITRATES, SELECTED RIVERS, 1965-1975

Index values

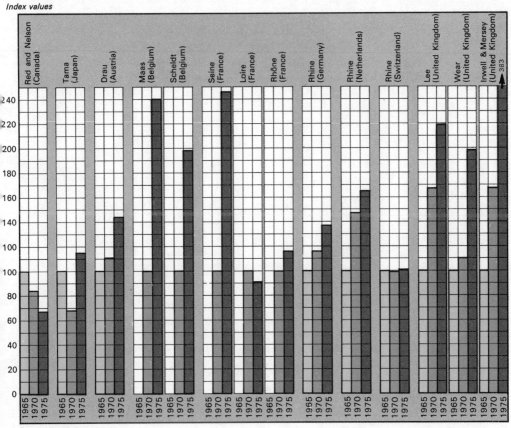

For details see Annex 19.

Figure 10

POLLUTION OF THE MEDITERRANEAN BY DOMESTIC SEWAGE AND INDUSTRIAL WASTE, 1974

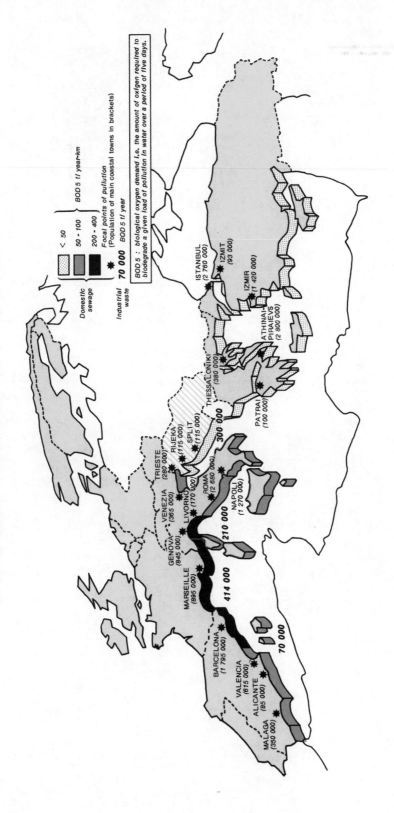

Fortunately the pollution of estuaries and coastal waters can to some extent be prevented, controlled or contained by dealing with the pollutants at source.

Accidental oil spills have occurred quite frequently (Table 9) and have received much public attention. The damage that results from oil thus spilled from ships or platforms, is usually local and of limited duration. However, the effects of exceptionally large spills, such as those from the Amoco Cadiz or Torrey Canyon, which led respectively to spillages of 230,000 and 117,000 tons, can persist for several years. The effects may include damage to fish, plankton, sea birds and other organisms. This leads in turn to the impairment of fishing and shellfish farming. These spills may also result in damage to beaches and shorelines leading to losses in the hotel and tourist trades and in amenities.

Although the probability of tanker accidents throughout the oceans is relatively low, the risk increases considerably where traffic is heavy. Moreover, as noted above, the damage is likely to be serious if accidents happen close to coasts where economic activities are concentrated. This is the case in the Channel, the North Sea, and along the United States Eastern Seaboard, all of which are important centres of fishing and tourism. Prevention, in the form of agreements on navigation, is increasingly seen as the best means of dealing with pollution from tanker accidents.

Although oil spills are often dramatic, land based sources of coastal pollution are much more significant. These include operations at terminals and in ports and also oily water discharges from off-shore platforms. Such discharges, because they take place constantly, can cause major changes in affected areas.

Table 9. SELECTED OIL SPILLS EXCEEDING 2,000 TONS IN MARINE WATERS,
OECD COUNTRIES, 1967-1979 [a]

YEAR	POLLUTER	AMOUNT OF OIL RELEASED TONS	AFFECTED AREA	TYPE OF ACCIDENT
1967	Torrey Canyon	117,000	UK/France	Went aground
1967	R.C. Stoner	20,000	North Pacific	Went aground
1968	Ocean Eagle	12,000	USA (Puerto Rico)	Went aground
1969	Santa Barbara Platform	6,000	USA (west coast)	Blew out
1970	Texaco Oklahoma	31,500	USA	Went aground
1970	Polycommandeur	16,000	Spain	Went aground
1970	Arrow	10,000	Canada (east coast)	Went aground
1970	Chevron Platform	10,000	USA (Mex. Gulf)	Caught fire
1970	Pacific Glory v. Allegro	6,300	United Kingdom	Collided
1970	Ocean Grandeur	2,500	Australia	Went aground
1971	Juliana	7,000	Japan	Went aground
1971	Oregon Standard	3,000	USA (west coast)	Collided
1973	Javvackta	16,000	Sweden	Went aground
1974	Mitzushima Refinery	8,000	Japan	Leaked
1974	Yuyo Maru	3,000	Japan	Collided
1974	Universe Leader	2,500	Ireland	Terminal Oper.
1974	Saglek	2,000	Canada (east coast)	Terminal Oper.
1975	Spartan Lady	20,000	North Atlantic	Sank
1975	Olympic Alliance v. HMS Achilles	2,100	United Kingdom	Collided
1975	Allied Chemical Barge	2,000	USA (east coast)	Sank
1976	Urquiola	100,000	Spain	Exploded
1976	Argo Merchant	25,000	USA (east coast)	Went aground
1976	Boelhen	10,000	France	Went aground
1976	Sealift Pacific	4,200	USA (Alaska)	Went aground
1976	Barge in Chesapeake Bay	2,700	USA (east coast)	Sank
1977	Grand Zenith	32,000	Canada (east coast)	Sank
1977	Ekofisk Platform	21,300	North Sea	Blew out
1977	Irenes Challenge	19,000	North Pacific	Sank
1978	Amoco Cadiz	230,000	France	Went aground
1978	Heleni V v. Roseline	4,000	United Kingdom	Collided
1979	Andros Patria	60,000	Spain	Caught fire
1979	Betelgeuse	35,000	Ireland	Terminal Oper.

NOTES:
a) January and February only for 1979.

Chapter 2

LAND

Land provides the base for virtually all human settlement and activities. It is a primary source of raw materials. It is also a component of the natural environment. Patterns of land use, the condition of the land, the protection of critical areas, and competition and conflicts between different users are therefore of major concern.

1. Changes in land use and land cover

Examination of patterns of land use by category in Member countries (Figure 11) reveals unsurprisingly wide variations.

The following changes are discernible over the past 20 years (Table 10):

- arable land is shrinking in nearly all European countries and in Japan while remaining stable or increasing in such less densely populated countries as Australia and New Zealand; even where total arable land is increasing, primary grade land may still be decreasing as in Canada;
- woodlands increased in European countries and showed stability for the OECD as a whole, though important changes have taken place in the varieties of trees grown and in the extent of management;
- built-up land tended to increase in all Member countries and in the two decades up to 1970 it grew by 25 per cent in the United States, 35 per cent in Germany, and 44 per cent in Belgium;
- permanent grassland showed stability in most countries.(1)

Underlying these overall trends lie wider shifts between land uses. Thus between 1967 and 1975 the conversion of prime farmland to urban development, highways, and other uses is estimated at 420,000 hectares a year in the United States alone. This annual loss is equivalent to about half the cultivated area of Norway. Conversion of land from farming to urban uses is also high in most

---

1) OECD (1976), "Land use policies and agriculture", Paris.

European countries and Japan (Annex 22). In Finland and Belgium the rate of loss of arable land nearly doubled during the 1950s and 1960s.

2.   The condition of land

An enormous variety of ecosystems, ranging from the deserts or semi-deserts of the United States and Australia to the ice fields of Canada and Norway are to be found in OECD countries. Within any ecosystem the condition of the land is shaped by a complex set of influences.

The condition of the land has been influenced, first of all, by the development of new farming and forestry practices. More specialised forms of cultivation, larger fields or changes in crops have generated changes in land cover and soil quality. In Sweden for instance the percentage of woodlands devoted to conifers has increased from 62 to 82 per cent in the last 25 years. In arid or semi-arid zones the rate of loss of topsoil has increased in recent years and may now amount to 50 tons of soil per year and per km^2 in some areas. In many countries, and especially in mountainous areas in Europe, marginal land is being abandoned. The extension of forests has occurred, at least in part, on such abandoned farm land. Changes of these kinds in turn modify the balance of ecosystems, influence wildlife habitats, and impose stresses on various forms of wildlife. For instance, the abandonment of cattle grazing in Swedish forests together with changed methods of forestry may be the main reasons for a radical increase in elk and roe deer.

A second influence on the condition of the land has been the extension of urban and industrial activities (Figure 12). There are also higher demands for land to accomodate new houses, roads and large civil engineering projects in suburban and rural areas and to provide tourist facilities in more remote country. The resultant coverage of land by tarmac and concrete is often irreversible. In particular, derelict land damaged by industrial or other urban developments is often abandoned, since it is incapable of being re-used without costly reclamation. In the United Kingdom damaged land of this type amounts to almost 1,000 km^2, while in the United States more than 10,000 km^2 of land are considered in need of reclamation.

Land can be damaged through improper waste disposal, dumping of public refuse or other materials. Land around factories and industrial waste disposal sites can be contaminated by toxic substances. In Japan 33 areas totalling about 4,000 ha have been designated as requiring clean-up effort including topsoil replacement and landscaping to eliminate the effects of contamination by cadmium, copper or arsenic. Disposal of wastes by landfill and by

66

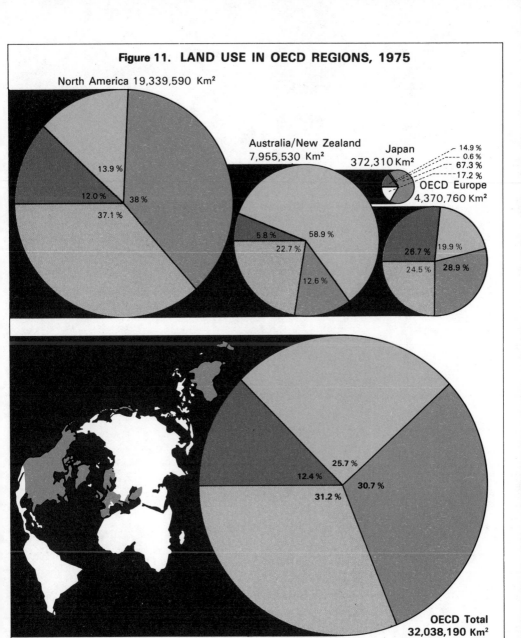

Figure 11. LAND USE IN OECD REGIONS, 1975

North America 19,339,590 Km²

Australia/New Zealand 7,955,530 Km²

Japan 372,310 Km²

OECD Europe 4,370,760 Km²

OECD Total 32,038,190 Km²

Regions	Arable and Crop Land		Permanent Grassland		Wooded Areas		Other Areas		Total Land
	Km²	%	Km²	%	Km²	%	Km²	%	Km²
North America	2,302,610	12.0	2,683,000	13.9	7,319,390	38.0	7,134,590	37.1	19,339,590
Australia/New Zealand	460,380	5.8	4,686,080	58.9	1,000,560	12.6	1,808,420	22.7	7,955,530
OECD Europe	1,164,000	26.7	872,950	19.9	1,262,100	28.9	1,071,810	24.5	4,370,760
Japan	55,720	14.9	2,420	0.6	250,430	67.3	63,740	17.2	372,310
OECD Total	3,982,710	12.4	8,244,350	25.7	9,832,570	30.7	9,978,560	31.2	32,038,190

For details see Annex 20.

Table 10. CHANGES IN LAND USE, OECD COUNTRIES, 1955-1975, BASE 100 IN 1955

COUNTRY	ARABLE AND CROP LAND [a]				PERMANENT GRASSLAND				WOODED AREA				OTHER AREAS			
	1960	1965	1970	1975	1960	1965	1970	1975	1960	1965	1970	1975	1960	1965	1970	1975
OECD Total	96.3	102.9	107.1	106.5	100.5	102	100.2	100.4	99.5	99.2	100	100	99.3	98.2	97.2	97.2
Canada	102.2	106.5	108.5	109.5	96.9	97	94.2	93.1	100.2	100.2	100.2	100.2	99.8	99.5	99.5	99.5
USA	97.7	96.3	101.0	101.0	100.1	100.4	95.3	95.3	97.9	96.0	95.0	94.0	105.5	109.9	113.7	115.4
Japan	101.5	100.4	96.9	93.2	100	100	100	100	101.6	102.2	100.1	101.1	91.4	89.8	102.4	110.5
Australia	128.2	160.3	194.5	194.4	101.5	103.9	104.7	105.5	100	100	100	100	94.0	85.8	80.8	79.2
New Zealand	107.8	124.1	141.2	144.2	100	100	100	100	100.8	101.6	102.9	103.4	98.5	96.3	93.5	92.8
Austria	99.1	98.3	93.1	88.6	99.4	97.6	95.8	94.4	100.6	101.7	102.6	104	100.7	104.7	109.1	114.1
Belgium	94.9	93.0	85.9	81.9	104.7	99.4	101.0	98.1	101.0	101.8	102.8	103.3	101.2	108.5	116.0	124.0
Denmark	101.7	99.2	98.0	97.8	87.5	82.9	76.2	70.6	102.9	105.6	106.9	107.6	98.9	108.8	115.8	119.1
Finland	103.4	106.4	103.9	102.9	63.9	48.7	31.0	56.5	100	100	100	100	100.1	99.8	100.7	100.4
France	101.1	96.4	90.2	89.6	105.8	109.0	112.9	108.6	100.8	107.1	121.1	125.8	89.3	87.8	77.8	78.9
Germany	97.6	93.4	92.6	92.4	100.9	101.3	97.3	92.8	100.8	101.9	101.7	101.6	102.7	111.0	120.0	125.4
Greece	102.8	106.9	104.6	102.2	98.4	95.4	94.2	94.2	102.0	106.8	108.9	109.3	94.7	88.3	88.4	87.4
Iceland	100	100	100	100	100	100	100	100	100	120	120	120	100	99.7	99.7	99.7
Ireland	100	89.4	92.9	101.3	95.4	103.8	105.1	103.5	113.6	165	197	212	106.4	95.6	89.7	86.3
Italy	99.7	95.8	92.2	75.4	98.3	99.3	101.5	102.2	101.1	105.7	106.9	109.4	96.8	99.2	101.5	140
Luxembourg	96.1	88.4	82.0	76.9	104.9	104.9	113.1	114.7	n.a.	102.3	104.6	105.8	100	112.5	106.2	115.6
Netherlands	98.8	92.2	81.7	79.5	101.7	103.2	107.0	100.2	110.0	118.8	123.4	129.3	106.8	109.8	120.3	134.7
Norway	102.0	102.4	98.4	95.7	91.7	78.1	67.9	51.4	99.9	99.9	118.4	118.4	100	100.2	94.9	95.2
Portugal	100	93.8	81.5	78.4	100	100	100	100	100	100	100	100	92.5	113.4	140	146.8
Spain	100.7	99.0	98.1	95.4	94.5	72.5 b	53.8 b	95.0	104.4	105.7	109.5	113.9	101.1	102.6	84.1	85.6
Sweden	95.4	85.1	80.9	79.7	100	100	103.1	93.9	100.0	101.4	101.4	100.6	101.4	103.7	104.2	103.7
Switzerland	96.7	91.3	86.3	85.9	91.6	98.5	94.5	94.5	101.6	101.4	100	107.2	99.5	98.7	100.1	109.2
Turkey	110.6	111.9	115.6	116.3	90.2	90.2	83.5	83.5	101.6	101.6	175	143.4	99.5	98.7	47.9	31.1
United Kingdom	102.9	104.3	101.4	98.0	102.2	98.5	94.5	94.5	105.3	111.8	118.3	125.1	83.1	87.8	108.0	112.3
Yugoslavia	101.8	101.0	99.6	97.2	100.1	98.3	97.9	96.9	100	101.3	102.1	103.4	92.4	94.9	97.6	103.3

NOTES:

a) Definitions and methods of measurement may differ between countries and different dates, "arable and crop land" is defined as the sum of arable area and of land under permanent crops, "other areas" includes urbanic land, desert, dunes, mountains, inland water ...

b) Uncertain figures due to difference in statistical procedures.

Figure 12
AREA OF BUILT-UP^a LAND IN OECD COUNTRIES, 1975

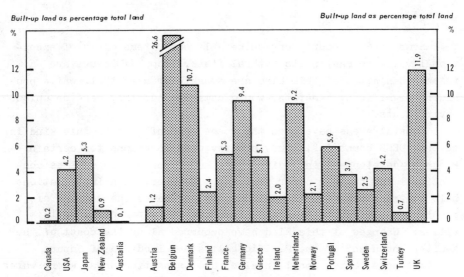

Built-up land as percentage total land

Built-up land as percentage total land

a) Built-up land is defined as land taken up by settlements, industry and transport.

For details see Annex 21.

Figure 13
POPULATION DENSITY RELATED TO THE HABITABLE^a AREA IN OECD COUNTRIES
mid-1970s

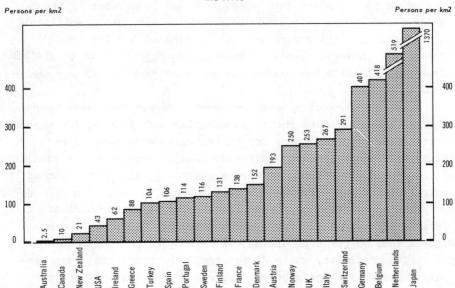

Persons per km2

Persons per km2

a) Habitable area is defined as the sum total of utilised and non utilised agricultural area and built-up area (see Annex 21).

For details see Annex 21.

burying is now becoming subject to control in an increasing number of countries.

3.   Critical land areas

Some land harbours very vulnerable ecosystems or is of exceptional value to man in its natural state. Complex issues are raised when sites of this kind are sought for uses that, while providing significant benefits, would damage or destroy rare or unique environments.

Coastal areas have been the scene of conflicts of this kind in several OECD countries. They are favoured locations for certain kinds of development including ports and industry, as well as conventional and nuclear power stations. However, such installations help to transform natural environments and cause the decline of fishing, shellfish farming and other coastal water-based activities. Changes of this kind have occurred along the coast of the Mediterranean and of the Pacific belt and Inland Sea of Japan.

Wetlands, often small in size, are transition areas where water and land come together. Within ecosystems, they stabilize water flows, provide sheltered habitats for wildlife and may also act as natural settling ponds for polluted waters. Wetlands have shrunk greatly in area. Over the past 50 years an average of 1,500 km^2 of them have been lost every year in the United States alone.

National parks have been long established in some countries, as a means to protect unique ecosystems and landscapes of beauty. In the decade up to 1975, they have nonetheless seen significant expansion in countries such as Canada, Finland and France (Table 11). Several countries have afforded protection to similar areas through their designation as regional parks which may include rural settings.

Sites that are of special cultural interest have also been acquired and managed by public authorities. In France, the number of protected areas amounts, for instance, to some 144,000 km^2 (areas with aesthetic and landscape value). Greater protection is afforded to 6,000 sites. In Europe generally, the protection of central cities has often been sought through the creation of pedestrian precincts and the designation of neighbourhoods of historic significance. Surveys conducted by OECD in 1977 demonstrated that 95 per cent of the cities sampled had implemented pedestrian precincts, while 74 per cent were protecting some central or residential neighbourhoods from the adverse effects of through traffic.

Large engineering projects and urban developments cause major changes to the condition of land and concerns about their impact on sensitive but unprotected areas have been growing. Such concerns

72

Table 11. NATIONAL AND REGIONAL PARKS, SELECTED COUNTRIES, 1965-1975

COUNTRY	NATIONAL AND REGIONAL PARKS Km^2			PERCENT OF COUNTRY IN NATIONAL AND REGIONAL PARKS %		
	1965	1970	1975	1965	1970	1975
Canada	78,834[a]	79,607[a]	316,380[b]	0.79[a]	0.79[a]	3.2[b]
USA[c]	144,523[d]	153,214	164,052[e]	1.5[d]	1.6	1.75[e]
Japan	49,306	49,793	51,760	12.4	13.4	13.9
Australia	..	27,905	42,993	..	0.36	0.60
New-Zealand[a]	20,510	20,570	21,537	7.6	7.7	8.0
Finland[f]	2,207	2,466	4,150	0.65	0.73	1.23
France[g]	1,990	15,158	29,112	0.4	2.8	5.3
Germany[h]	17,501	34,320	39,927[b]	7.0	13.8	16.1[b]
Greece	..	2,501	6,406[i]	..	1.9	4.9[i]
Netherlands[a]	67	113	113	0.18	0.31	0.31
Norway[a]	1,659	2,079	5,047	0.5	0.6	1.6
Portugal[h]	..	753	813	..	0.84	0.91
Sweden[a]	6,178	6,178	6,178	1.4	1.4	1.4
Turkey[a]	224	527	2,349	0.03	0.07	0.30
United Kingdom	..	21,550	..	..	8.8	..

NOTES: Comparisons between countries should be avoided due to differences in definitions of protected areas and extent of protection.

a) National Parks only.

b) Total including National Parks (1975) and Regional Parks (1976).

c) Regional Parks include state parks but not local (county, city) parks.

d) Total including National Parks (1965) and Regional Parks (1967).

e) Total including National Parks (1976) and Regional Parks (1975).

f) These are strictly conserved areas, and include National Parks and National Forest Reserves.

g) Total including National Parks (peripheric zone included) (1975), and Regional Parks (1977).

h) Column 1970 refers to 1971 data.

i) These are totally protected areas and can be considered as wildlife refuges and wilderness preservation areas as well as National and Regional Parks.

73

stem from reinforced knowledge regarding the fragility of the natural environment and an awareness of the increasing pressures that are being exerted on it by such factors in human life as high density settlements, quest for mobility and preferences for living in coastal areas.

Experience in the management of land as a resource has been acquired at the scale of cities and national parks. Recently there have been calls to expand the breadth of such environmentally conscious management of land and to undertake systematic assessments of the environmental consequences of urban and industrial developments.(1)

4. Land use concerns

Increasing human activity has led to a sharpening of competition for land between different uses. For example, space devoted to tourism has increased by 40,000 km^2 in the United States and 16,000 km^2 in Europe over the past ten years. This growth has occurred often in environmentally sensitive coastal or mountain areas and at the expense of farming or forestry. Modern farming and forestry have in turn tended to destroy at least part of the countryside's attractiveness for tourists.

Competition at the international level is likewise leading to land use specialisation that has significant implications for the environment. For example, the South European and Alpine countries "export" large amounts of land devoted to tourism and recreation to their North European neighbours. Likewise, feed imported into the Netherlands for livestock would, if grown locally, require two-thirds of the country's farmland. In the United States, an area larger than the agricultural land of France is "exported" every year in the form of cereals.

One possible answer to increased competition for land is multiple use. In certain areas, it may be possible for farming and tourism to co-exist. Land may also be used for different purposes at different times of year.

Yet the competition for land is often so keen that direct conflicts result. For instance, this has happened in connection with the creation of an expressway in the western suburbs of Paris, the opening of Narita airport near Tokyo and the siting of pipelines in Canada. The exclusiveness of many land uses and their economic potential in other uses can create situations in which there is often no alternative but arbitration. This has stimulated the

---

1) OECD Recommendation on "The Analysis of the Environmental Consequences of Significant Public and Private Projects", 14th November, 1974.

development of mechanisms such as environmental impact assessment
procedures, public inquiries or hearings designed to reconcile
local and national concerns, as well as conflicting public and private interests.

Chapter 3

<u>AIR</u>

1. <u>Air quality: an overview</u>

Air pollution was perceived as a major problem in some countries as early as the 1950s, though in others not until the late 1960s. Initially it was seen as a phenomenon consisting of high concentrations of a few well known pollutants such as particulate matter, sulphur dioxide and carbon monoxide that were found primarily in urban and industrial areas, and that caused easily identifiable effects, such as ill-health, loss of visibility or soiling.

Action, where taken, helped to curb emissions and to eliminate very high concentrations of pollutants. All this was done at a relatively low cost by adapting products and processes of production and use. It was also achieved despite a continuing rapid growth in various human activities that were generating the perceived pollutants.

During this period intensive study revealed a range of other air pollutants, such as nitrogen oxides, hydrocarbons, photochemical oxidants, sulphate, nitrates and fine particulates. Knowledge increased with respect to the transformation and transport of chemicals in the atmosphere. Finally, theories began to emerge about the way in which different substances interacted in the atmosphere to acquire added toxicity or to form secondary substances. Furthermore, actions effective in reducing acute damage to health by some pollutants, such as carbon monoxide, sulphur dioxide and smoke, were observed to be less effective in improving visibility, lessening damage to materials and in avoiding long-term adverse effects on health. Work today is therefore focused on understanding the newly identified problems and finding ways of dealing with them.

A first objective of this endeavour is to improve monitoring networks, so that they are capable of producing more precise and detailed information. This would lead to better measurements of the ways in which air pollutants affect human health and vegetation and how they corrode materials.

2.   Air pollution by sulphur dioxide and particulates

Sulphur dioxide and particulate matter have been recognised as major pollutants in urban areas for more than two decades. Their control was often joined because of early suspicions that their effects were augmented when they appeared together.

Sulphur compounds affect human health, plants, trees, rivers, lakes and building materials. Emissions of sulphur dioxide increased in all OECD countries during the 1960s because more coal and oil were burned. Depending upon the structure of the country, total emission levels per unit of energy consumed varied in 1975 from highs in Canada and in the United Kingdom to lows in Norway and the Netherlands. The upward trend was reversed in a number of OECD countries in the 1970s and a reduction of over one-half in SO_2 emissions was achieved in Japan between 1970 and 1975 (Figure 14). Sulphur dioxide emissions per unit of energy used have in general decreased even more significantly than total emissions (Figure 15). A recent OECD study shows that for OECD as a whole such emissions from fuel combustion were at about the same level in 1974 as in 1968, although energy use had continued to grow.[1]

These results can be attributed to: slower economic growth plus increased energy conservation and therefore a slower rate of growth in energy use; greater use of natural gas in some countries and increased use of low sulphur content crude oil; as well as rapid growth in the use of scrubbers and other techniques for the removal of sulphur. Differences in economic structure, in industrial activities and in emission controls account, however, for substantial variations in air pollution and its abatement in different countries.

One of the main aims of pollution abatement policies has been to reduce the exposure of the population to high concentrations of sulphur dioxide. With few exceptions this has been achieved and in many cities where concentrations of sulphur dioxide were high, they have now declined (Table 12). Reviews of national trends for Japan and the United States show favourable results in these two countries. Available estimates of the people exposed to outdoor concentrations of sulphur dioxide, exceeding locally specified levels, in certain study areas in 1970 and 1975 give further confirmation of the generally downward trend (Annex 26). Better control of emissions, the use of high stacks designed to disperse pollutants, as well as in some countries the location of industry away from urban areas, explain these results. The total sulphur dioxide discharge into the atmosphere has not only been reduced but also often more widely dispersed. Conflicting views exist as to whether the dispersion of sulphur dioxide is a sufficient answer to the problem.

1) OECD (1978) "Clean Fuel Supply".

Figure 14.
Figure 14. TOTAL EMISSIONS OF SULPHUR DIOXIDE (SO₂), SELECTED COUNTRIES, 1965-1975

Index values 1970 = 100

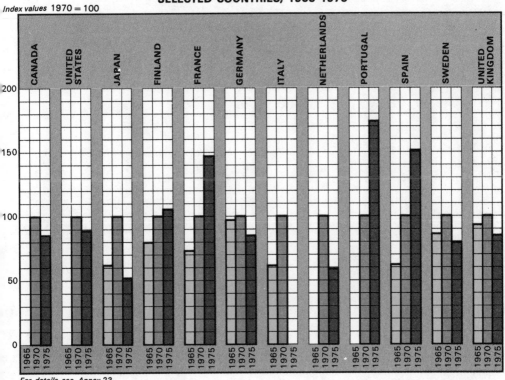

For details see Annex 23.

79

Figure 15. EMISSIONS OF SULPHUR DIOXIDE (SO$_2$) PER UNIT OF ENERGY CONSUMED, SELECTED COUNTRIES, 1965-1975

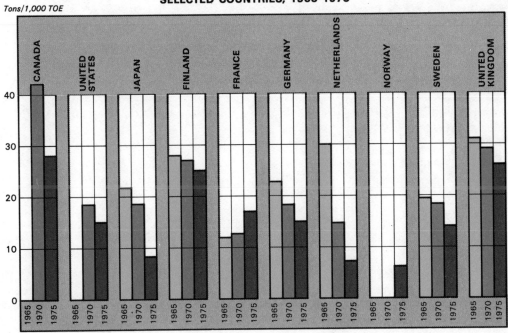

For details see Annex 25.

Table 12. ANNUAL MEAN DAILY CONCENTRATIONS (a) OF SULPHUR DIOXIDE (SO₂), SELECTED URBAN AND INDUSTRIAL AREAS, 1970-1976

Table 12. ANNUAL MEAN DAILY CONCENTRATIONS (a) OF SULPHUR DIOXIDE (SO_2), SELECTED URBAN AND INDUSTRIAL AREAS, 1970-1976

Urban or industrial areas	1970	1971	1972	1973	1974	1975	1976
CANADA							
Montréal	100	69	57	38	37	36	29
Toronto	100	69	45	30	30	26	25
UNITED STATES (b)							
New England	100	90	78	69	71	75	65
Great Lakes	100	91	89	76	59	69	62
JAPAN							
Tokyo	100	62	55	64	55	49	47
Osaka	100	75	54	42	34	40	32
Nagoya	..	100	84	63	47	40	35
BELGIUM							
Brussels	..	100	91	79	67	62	63
Antwerp	100	95	94	101	81	75	58
Ghent	100	106	91	102	78	68	75
FRANCE							
Paris	100	105	119	128	95	99	100
Lyons	100	154	152	140	115	104	108
Marseilles	100	101	91	92	67	71	82
GERMANY							
Gelsenkirchen	100	76	79	78	76	78	66
Mannheim	100	55	25	25	40	..	..
Frankfurt/M.	100	125	97	97	96	95	88
LUXEMBOURG (c)	..	..	100	93	65	60	58
PORTUGAL							
Lisbon	100	100	120	85	56	92	113
SPAIN							
Madrid	100	101	84	108	98	85	76
Barcelona	100	96	68	61	42	56	..
Bilbao	100	101	104	112	128	135	122
SWEDEN							
Gothenburg	100	43	38	67	62	62	..
UNITED KINGDOM (d)							
London	100	105	89	89	74	78	71
N.W. Region	100	97	78	74	72	66	70

(a) Measured in μg/m³, based 100 in 1970. In studying trends shown it is important to take into account the fact that annual changes in the weather pattern can easily mask the effect of a 25 % change in the emissions.
(b) 60 sites in 6 states in North Eastern USA, 160 sites in 6 states surrounding the Great Lakes.
(c) Average of measures throughout the country network.
(d) Data for different years do not necessarily refer to the same measurement sites; N.W. Region includes Manchester and Merseyside.

Considerable efforts have been made to control emissions of particulate matter not only because of the annoyance they cause but because of their effect on health when combined with sulphur dioxide. Trends in emissions of such pollutants over the period 1970-1975 show a greater decrease than for sulphur dioxide in a number of OECD countries (Annex 23). Emissions have been cut by about one-half in Germany and France. Smoke has been reduced to the same extent in the United Kingdom and emissions of all forms of particles have been reduced by more than 30 per cent in the United States.

Decreases in the exposure of people to particulate matter have also been recorded in several countries and particularly in the more severely polluted areas (Annex 26). In the United States the proportion of a large sample of people exposed to levels potentially hazardous to health fell from 45 per cent in 1970 to 28 per cent in 1975. In the United Kingdom the hours during which sunshine penetrated to the ground in central London and Manchester in the winter have been rising. In Japan, dust fall has decreased significantly, although concentrations of dust particles, light enough to float in the air, remain above health standards at the majority of monitoring stations. Improvements in air quality in the United Kingdom are due mainly to domestic smoke control. In many other countries decreases in emissions and in ambient concentrations are the result of increased use of industrial emission control equipment. Such equipment can effectively collect coarse particles, over 2-3 microns in diameter. It does not, however, eliminate finer particulates. The result is a decrease in the total volume of particulate emissions, but an increase in the emission of fine particulates.(1) This fine dust can be deposited in lungs, causing bronchitis, impaired breathing and increased susceptibility to asthma and the common cold. It also affects visibility and climatic temperature.

During the last 10 years, it has been generally recognised that sulphur dioxide and particulate matter, in addition to being pollutants in themselves, react chemically and physically in the atmosphere. In particular they combine and then form aerosols or minute quantities of solid or liquid matter dispersed throughout the air. The resulting pollutants affect health, reduce visibility and cause acid rain. Recent field studies in the United States show that sulphur dioxide in power plant fumes is converted to sulphates in the course of travelling over distances of 100 to 500 km and may affect wide areas.(2) The fine particles fall only slowly to the

---

1) EEC Seminar on Fine Particulates, Villach, Austria, 17th - 22nd October, 1977.
2) US-EPA (1978), "Research Outlook".

Table 13. ESTIMATED DEPOSITION OF SULPHUR[a], EUROPE, 1974

RECEIVERS \ EMITTERS	AUSTRIA	BELGIUM	DENMARK	FINLAND	FRANCE	GERMANY	ITALY	NETHERLANDS	NORWAY	SWEDEN	SWITZERLAND	UNITED KINGDOM AND IRELAND	OTHER AREAS[c]	UNATTRIBUTED	TOTAL[a] RECEIVED FROM ALL AREAS	ANNUAL EMISSION 1973
Austria	60	6	0	0	20	40	30	2	0	0	5	20	67	30	300	221
Belgium	0	100	0	0	30	20	0	5	0	0	0	30	6	10	200	499
Denmark	0	1	60	0	3	6	0	1	0	2	0	10	11	10	100	312
Finland	2	2	8	100	4	10	0	2	2	30	6	10	137	70	400	274
France	8	40	1	0	600	50	30	10	0	0	6	100	57	150	1,000	1,616
Germany	0	60	7	0	100	700	7	40	0	2	7	100	120	90	1,300	1,964
Netherlands	0	10	1	0	10	10	0	60	0	0	0	30	6	10	150	391
Norway	0	4	8	1	9	30	0	4	30	9	0	60	22	100	250	91
Sweden	0	7	30	10	10	30	0	6	6	100	0	40	108	100	500	415
Switzerland	1	2	2	0	20	7	6	1	0	0	30	10	6	20	100	76
United Kingdom ..	0	8	0	0	20	10	0	4	0	0	0	800	14	100	1,000	2,883[b]
Other Areas[c]	60	60	80	40	200	400	900	40	9	50	10	600	700	1,000	11,000	..
Total emitted to above areas[a]	100	300	200	150	1,000	1,300	1,000	200	40	200	60	1,800	8,200	1,900	17,000	n.a.

NOTES:

a) Unit: 10^3 tons of sulphur. These data are based on 1973 emission data. The 1974 meteorological conditions are used to calculate the 1974 sulphur deposition. Number rounded to one significant figure and accurate to within ± 50%. The sums are calculated from unrounded figures and thereafter rounded separately.

b) Including 80,000 tons of sulphur from Ireland.

c) Other areas refer to some other European countries not included in the list of either the emitting countries or the receiving countries.

ground and can be transported in significant quantities over distances of several thousand kilometres. Over North-Eastern Europe and large parts of North America they frequently form layers of continuous haze, measurably reducing visibility at and above ground levels. The particles are usually a dark mixture of acidic sulphates, soot and flyash, more or less neutralised by ammonia emitted from the land. However, if the polluted air masses remain over extensive water bodies, particles of highly acid sulphates can be formed which in turn can for example acidify lakes. As both sulphur dioxide and sulphate aerosols dissolve in water, precipitation clears them from the atmosphere.

Measurements of sulphate levels in the United States support this observation.[1] Sulphate concentrations in cities East of the Mississippi tend to be high, with the highest readings recorded in cities lying in the strip from New York to Chicago. Studies by OECD of long range transport of air pollutants in Europe show that sulphur is carried across frontiers.[2] Where both sulphur dioxide and sulphate aerosols were transported over distances up to a few thousand kilometres they contributed to the acidity of rain and other precipitation. A first estimate of the relative importance of sulphur deposition of national and foreign origin may therefore be made using data collected in 1974 (Table 13). Investigations in 1975 and 1976 show the importance of changes in the weather, particularly the wind, in the contributions made by countries of origin to the long range transport of pollutants.

Efforts to reduce urban levels of sulphur dioxide and particulate matter have thus been generally successful. The emission of fine sulphate particles, their transport over long distances and their low level effects over wide areas continues. Complex and less well understood interactions with other substances and possible synergistic effects may also be occurring.

3. Air pollution by carbon monoxide

Carbon monoxide was early recognised to have adverse effects on health. It impairs the capacity of the blood to absorb oxygen, reducing physical performance and affecting the nervous system.

Carbon monoxide is mainly the result of the incomplete combustion of fuel by motor vehicles. During the period 1970 to 1975 decreases in total emissions were recorded in the United States and Canada while increases occurred in Finland, France, Sweden and Switzerland (Annex 23). During the same period vehicle ownership

---

1) US-EPA (1978), "Research Outlook".
2) OECD (1977), "Long-Range Transport of Air Pollutants".

and use grew considerably in many countries. The implementation of progressively more stringent standards for new cars was the main cause for the reduced emissions. The emission standards are generally stricter and older in Japan and the United States than in Europe and Australia. The best available technology is capable of reducing carbon monoxide emissions by 80 per cent compared with uncontrolled vehicles and technology planned for the early 1980s may reduce them by 95 per cent. However, emissions generally increase with vehicle age and are heavily dependent upon driving patterns and on the quality and frequency of engine maintenance. An average vehicle with today's best technology will probably reduce emissions over a 10 year lifetime by 60 per cent rather than the theoretical maximum of 80 per cent.[1] The replacement of old vehicles by new ones thus results in progressive action against carbon monoxide though this benefit may be offset by increases in vehicle numbers and the amount they are used.

High ambient levels of carbon monoxide may be found in cities but levels vary in space and time since vehicles are concentrated in central areas and along heavily used main roads, especially during peak traffic periods. Reductions in concentrations have been measured in Japan and North America.[2] A programme of inspection and maintenance in New Jersey produced notable reductions between 1972 and 1977 despite increases in fuel consumption. These programmes are based on measuring the percentage of carbon monoxide emitted by vehicle engines while they are idling and they have been effective where used in Europe, North America and Japan. In some countries traffic management and diversion schemes, involving pedestrian areas and traffic cells, have produced reductions of up to two-thirds in local carbon monoxide concentrations.[3]

Pollution by carbon monoxide is being contained by the use of emission control technology in those countries where action has been taken to reduce it. Inspection and maintenance and traffic management may be needed in parts of some cities to supplement such controls.

---

1) OECD (1978), "The Cost and Effectiveness of Automotive Exhaust Emissions Control Regulations", Paris.

2) In Japan, CO-emissions have declined in major cities since 1969 and in 1975 ambient air quality standards were achieved for nearly all residential monitoring stations and for 80 per cent of the roadside stations. In the United States CO-levels over the period 1970-1976 were reduced at about 80 per cent of the sampling locations, with higher rates of decline for California, which has stronger exhaust emission standards.

3) OECD (1975), "Better Towns with Less Traffic"; OECD (1979), "Managing Transport".

4. Nitrogen oxides, hydrocarbons and photochemical oxidants

In the atmosphere nitrogen oxide is rapidly oxidised to form NO_2, a toxic gas that decomposes in sunlight and begins a series of complex reactions that can, in the presence of hydro-carbons, result in "photochemical oxidants" such as ozone and peroxyacetylnitrate (PAN). Gaseous or particulate nitrates are formed in these reactions in amounts that contribute to the acidity of rain, dew and other forms of precipitation.

Emissions of nitrogen oxides (Figure 16 and Figure 17) increased in many places between 1970 and 1975. They increased in Japan, Canada, the United States, in Finland, France, Germany, the Netherlands, and Sweden. In the United Kingdom no changes were recorded. The increases were due to a greater use of motor vehicles and to the fact that emission standards were only recently introduced. Increases were also due to the growth in the number and size of stationary sources. Decreases in emissions on the other hand were observed after 1974 in Japan. A stabilization or decrease in emissions were also found in the United States, as a result of slower economic growth and fuel conservation.

The deterioration-in-use of current systems for controlling nitrogen oxide emissions from vehicles results in a lifetime efficiency only 10 per cent greater than no control at all. Furthermore, to date the motor service industry has found no techniques or equipment to enable deterioration to be corrected.

Ambient levels of nitrogen oxides can vary considerably, depending on the day, the season and the weather. Those currently found in most cities are, with the exception of Los Angeles and a few Japanese cities, at or below those proposed by the World Health Organisation. In Japan nitrogen oxides tended to increase up to 1974 and then levelled off or began to fall: in the United States no clear trends have been identified.

Hydrocarbons are the best known for their role in the formation of photo-chemical oxidants. They are among the most difficult air pollutants to control because they are emitted where-ever fuel is handled or burned. Many of them are a key component in almost all atmospheric reactions. Gaseous hydrocarbons are furthermore toxic or causes of cancer, though not at the concentrations measured in city air. They can, by absorption or reaction, become fine particles capable of being inhaled.

Records show that over the period 1970-1975, total emissions of hydrocarbons increased in Norway, Sweden and the United Kingdom and remained stable, or decreased slightly in Germany, the Netherlands, Canada, and the United States (Annex 23). The increases are explained by higher emissions from sources such as fuel handling and the use of solvents for which little or no control technology is or

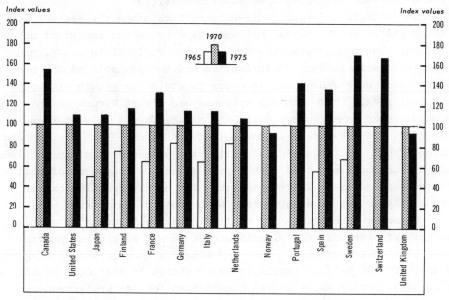

Figure 16

TOTAL EMISSION OF NITROGEN OXIDES (NO$_x$)
selected countries, 1965-1975, base 100 in 1970

For details see Annex 23.

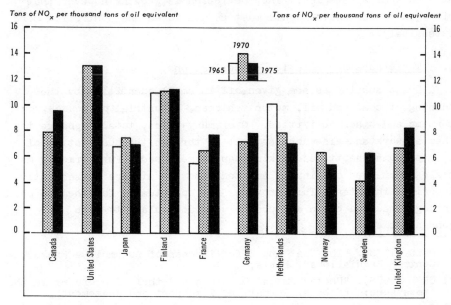

Figure 17

EMISSIONS OF NITROGEN OXIDES (NO$_x$) PER UNIT OF ENERGY CONSUMED
selected countries, 1965-1975

For details see Annex 25.

can be used. Such increases are not compensated for in all countries by the 30 to 70 per cent reduction in lifetime hydrocarbon emissions from motor vehicles of 1977 or later models.(1)

In Australia, Japan, South-Eastern Canada and the Western United States photochemical oxidants have become an important urban problem. The phenomenon, however, is also regional in scale, and observations in Eastern North America and Europe indicate the need for control over wide areas in order to avoid the growth of photochemical smog. Photochemical oxidants are always formed in the atmosphere on sunny summer days, and may be formed in winter as in the case of a snow storm in Quebec City in March 1977. The amounts formed depend on the sun's intensity, the presence of nitrogen oxides and hydrocarbons and to a much lesser extent on transport of pollutants over medium to long distances. The highly reactive oxidants are easily broken down on contact with other pollutants.

Networks of stations for monitoring ambient levels of nitrogen oxide, hydrocarbons and oxidants are of recent origin and provide only limited information. They nevertheless suggest that during the summer of 1976 oxidant levels in major cities in most OECD countries were considerably above levels recommended for the protection of public health.(2)(3) Reductions in oxidants levels have been registered in Japan since 1973, and also for cities in California in recent years. In Europe no trends emerge from available data. However as the weather is the dominant factor causing high oxidant levels, data are needed over five years to correlate ambient levels with control strategies. The conviction is growing however that nitrogen oxides and oxidants must be monitored and controlled more extensively.

5. Toxic substances in low concentration

Toxic substances are given off in small quantities by the burning of coal and oil, motor vehicles, industrial processes, farming and other activities. Over many years, total exposure to them at work and elsewhere as well as through the observation of such personal habits as smoking can be measured. Furthermore, many toxic substances originally emitted into the air are subsequently deposited in water. This provides the opportunity for them to pass through the food chain and possibly to accumulate to high concentrations.

1) OECD (1978), "The Cost and Effectiveness of Automotive Exhaust Control Regulations", Paris,
2) OECD (1978), "Photochemical Oxidants and their Precursors in the Atmosphere: Effects, Formation, Transport and Abatement".
3) 0.05 to 0.10 ppm one hour mean O_3 concentration not to be exceeded more than once per month (WHO).

Emissions, ambient air levels and the transport and transformation of toxic substances such as nickel, asbestos, cadmium, mercury, lead, beryllium, vanadium, vinyl chloride, benzo-a-pyrene, several halogenated organics and benzene have been measured in some countries. Little of this monitoring has been continuous. Nevertheless data are available that show decreases in the concentration of lead, nickel, chromium, vanadium and cadmium in some American cities since 1965. Several countries have monitored trace elements in the air and in rainfall and have generally found them contained in fine particulates. They are also known to travel over long distances in considerable quantities. Analyses of Greenland ice layers confirm this for tetraethyl lead. Many halogenated organic compounds also travel long distances through the atmosphere.

Many of the toxic substances named above cause cancer, genetic changes and deformities at birth. The points at which long-term exposure to low concentrations of them affect human health remain to be discovered.

6. Other problems

During the past few years there has been increasing agreement on the need for additional research into the potential long-term effect of air pollution on ecosystems, climate and the stratosphere. Changes in the characteristics of soils due to leaching by acid precipitation and changes in large bodies of water due to toxic substances could result in ecological effects. Increased concentrations of carbon dioxide and other pollutants could cause a rise in global air temperature or "greenhouse effect" leading to changes in precipitation affecting croplands and deserts. Sulphates and other fine particulates that affect visibility could also reduce solar radiation. Finally, halocarbons, in particular freon, nitric oxide from supersonic jets and nitrous oxide may cause depletion of the ozone layer of the atmosphere.

Effects on ecosystems

Rain and other precipitation over Scandinavia and Eastern North America has become more acid as a result of long range transport of sulphur dioxide, sulphates and nitrates.[1][2] So far no effect has been found in the growth of vegetation, though there are indications that forests may be affected.[3] Acid fall-out however has serious

---

1) OECD (1977), "Long Range Transport of Air Pollutants".
2) NILU (1978), "Planning Conference on the Long Range Transport of Oxidants and their Precursors", Oslo.
3) OECD Workshop on Plant Damage from SO_2.

and immediate effects on life in lakes and rivers. Evidence from some areas of Sweden shows that acidification can give rise to serious environmental problems which require action against the sources of the pollutants. Elsewhere the liming of lakes may be sufficient. In Scandinavia the Baltic Commission is monitoring the fall-out of heavy metals since there is a suspicion that the atmosphere may be contributing significantly to pollutants found in the sea.(1)

Effects on climate

Data from Sweden, Australia, Alaska and Hawaii in the United States show that carbon dioxide is increasing in the atmosphere. Increases from about 280 parts per million in 1880 to 330 parts per million in 1976 have been found and over the past 20 years increases have been at the rate of almost one part per million per year. This may be due to carbon dioxide from the burning of fossil fuels and to a fall in the global absorption of carbon dioxide by vegetation due to a worldwide shrinkage in forests. As carbon dioxide even at low concentrations absorbs infra-red radiation from the earth, it plays an important role in controlling the climate. Not enough is known about the relationship between changes in the rate at which fossil fuels are burnt and levels of carbon monoxide in the atmosphere.

Sulphates and other fine particles, generally measuring from 0.1 to 1.0 microns, scatter light and so interfere with visibility and radiation from the sun. They also may affect climate but, as with carbon monoxide, little is known about the relationship between the rates of burning of fossil fuels, levels of industrial activity, emissions of sulphates and other fine particles and their effects on visibility and climate.

Effects on the stratosphere

World production of fluorocarbons grew from about 100,000 to more than 1,000,000 metric tons metween 1970 and 1974. OECD countries produced about 80 per cent of this amount, mainly for use as aerosol propellants, refrigerants and solvents.(2) Chlorofluorocarbons, a set of related compounds, have the potential to deplete the ozone layer that shields the earth's surface from excessive exposure to ultraviolet radiation. A significant depletion of this shield would therefore be harmful to people and the biosphere. There is uncertainty about the rate at which depletion is happening

---

1) International Baltic Marine Environment Protection Commission working papers, 1977.

2) OECD (1976), "Fluorocarbons: an Assessment of Worldwide Production, Use and Environmental Issues".
   OECD (1978), "The Economic Impact of Restrictions on the Use of Fluorocarbons".

but steps have been taken to reduce the release of fluorocarbons
by developing substitutes for them and restricting their use to
closed systems. Several Member countries have for instance reduced
their use in spray cans. Improved understanding of ozone depletion
and its effects on climate and the biosphere also depends in part on
monitoring the levels of compounds such as methylchloroform, freon-22
and chloroform in the stratosphere.

Chapter 4

WILDLIFE

Ninety per cent of the world's food come from only 12 species
of plants, although many thousand species are believed to be edible.
Such biological diversity in plants and animals provides a pool of
genes on which breeders can draw. It is also a stock likely to have
undiscovered potential.

Large numbers of wild animals and wild plants are also used for
biomedical research and health care. In the case of primates, for
instance, some 90,000 are used every year, mainly for drug testing
which is often required by law or regulations.

Plant products are used in industry to make gum, latex, camphor
and resins and they are sources of oils, food colouring and spices.
Whales and manatees provide a high quality grade of industrial oil.
Animals such as alligators and many fur-bearing mammals are hunted
for their skins and furs. Other industrial products may remain to
be discovered. Indeed, it was only one hundred years ago that the
value of the rubber tree was recognised, and the biological resources
of the sea have received even less screening and testing than those
of the land.

1.   The Condition of Wildlife[1]

Historical records of animals that have become extinct are
incomplete and available statistics are sketchy. It appears however
that more than half the known animal extinctions of the last 2,000
years have occurred since 1900 and that the rate is rising. The
International Union for the Conservation of Nature estimates that
one animal species or subspecies is lost every year.

Governments and private organisations have tried to slow the
rate of extinction by declaring certain species to be endangered or
threatened and then adopting measures to protect them.[2] The
numbers and kinds of species that are endangered or threatened vary

---

1) The condition of wildlife has three aspects: the number or
   diversity of species measured over decades or centuries; the
   population of given species measured over years or decades; and
   the functioning of ecosystems.

2) An endangered species is generally agreed to be one that is in
   danger of extinction throughout all or a significant part of its
   natural habitat. A threatened species is one that is likely to
   become endangered in the foreseeable future.

Table 14.   ENDANGERED OR THREATENED SPECIES, SELECTED COUNTRIES, 1975

SPECIES	UNITED STATES[a]			EUROPE		
	TOTAL NUMBER OF SPECIES	NUMBER OF ENDANGERED OR THREATENED SPECIES	PERCENTAGE OF SPECIES ENDANGERED OR THREATENED	TOTAL NUMBER OF SPECIES	NUMBER OF ENDANGERED OR THREATENED SPECIES	PERCENTAGE OF SPECIES ENDANGERED OR THREATENED
Vegetal species	..	..	10	14,000	1,400[b]	10
Bird species	800	65	8	407	220	54[c]
Mammal species	400	36	9	156	36	23
Reptiles and Amphibians ..	460	12	3	150	64	43[d]
Fishes (freshwater)	660	39	6	..	..	..

NOTES:

a)   1977.

b)   Rare or threatened.

c)   1970, species declining in number.

d)   Does not cover asian part of Turkey.

SOURCE: For United States: Council of Environmental Quality (1975), "Environmental Quality";   US Department of the Interior (1976), "Endangered
Species Technical Bulletin, september 1976";
For Europe: OECD estimates based on Council of Europe Surveys and Yeatman, "Histoire des Oiseaux d'Europe".

widely among countries and regions (Table 14). In the United States, there are approximately 400 species of mammals of which close to 9 per cent are listed as endangered or threatened. In OECD Europe about 23 per cent of the 156 species of mammals are listed as endangered or threatened, although many large predator mammals have already become extinct.

There is also evidence that in some areas the population of a large number of species is in decline, although few are endangered. In Europe, for instance, it is estimated that of 407 species of birds, 220 are decreasing in number, 62 are stable, and 126 are growing. Habitat changes appear to explain the decline of 56 species, pollution another 12, and voluntary killing a further 80. The main cause of growth of 18 species appears to be protection by humans.

These trends reflect the development of man's activities and their impact on ecosystems. Hunting and fishing, changes in wildlife habitats and the introduction of polluting substances in the environment appear to be the major influences on the condition of wildlife.

2.   Impacts on Wildlife[1]

Hunting, Fishing, and Collection

Large numbers of people fish and hunt in OECD countries (Annex 27). In the Netherlands, Norway, Sweden, Finland and the United States, the number licenced to fish ranges from 6 to 15 per cent of the population. In France, Finland, the United States and Canada, those licenced to hunt range from 3 to 11 per cent. Levels of registered participation in the smaller and more densely populated European countries and Japan are lower though, as might be expected, and fishing is more widely practiced than hunting. Commercial harvesting often imposes far greater pressure on wildlife than hunting and fishing by individuals.

The elimination since 1600 of 33 per cent of all mammal species and 42 per cent of all birds is believed to be due largely to overkilling. It is responsible for the present plight of large numbers of threatened birds, reptiles and fish species.

One form of overkill is the deliberate killing or removal of predators such as wolves, bears, lions, and other large mammals. In the case of the American red and lobo wolves, restrictions on killing came about only after it was discovered that both were endangered species.

---

1) Wildlife may be adversely affected by selective actions, which include hunting, fishing, collecting wildlife for research, and the direct application of pesticides. It may also suffer from non-selective actions which, while less easily identified are probably more important in the long run. These include damage to habitats and the broadcasting of polluting substances.

The maintenance of stocks of game depends on the limitation of annual killings to a level balanced by reproductive capacity. The adoption of such an objective tends to result in the improved management and protection of wild animals and the improved organisation of hunting.

Game reserves, which are particularly effective in increasing the protection of large mammals, mountain game and waterfowl can be complemented by other actions such as the establishment of hunting plans, control over the rearing of game and the protection of rural and forest environments. Hunting regulations have also been strengthened and enforced in several countries.

A case of overkill can be found in the recent history of the whale. After 1945 whaling became highly mechanised with whalers able to search out and kill large numbers of animals using explosive-tipped harpoons. As the larger blue and fin whales were depleted, the industry turned to smaller whales, continuing the process until today 8 species have become endangered.[1] Despite the efforts of the International Whaling Commission and some national governments to protect whales, there is evidence of a continued fall in numbers. Such decline affects many stocks of whales, and most species that have been drastically reduced show no signs of recovery.

Statistics show that the worldwide catch of fish[1] levelled off after 1973 (Figure 2), and this tendency reflects the vulnerability of commercially acceptable fish stocks. Overfishing has in several cases destroyed or diminished some fish resources, thereby changing the balance between different components of the aquatic environment. Efforts are being made and some progress has been recorded with the management of fish resources.

Habitat Modification

The most important reason for the decline of wildlife is the loss or alteration of natural habitats, largely as a result of mining, forestry, urbanisation, transport, and above all agricultural practices. These activities take many forms, but often lead to the alteration of diversified landcover supporting many forms of inter-related plant and animal life and to the destruction or depletion of nesting areas and food supplies.

A few large areas of natural wilderness remain in the United States, Canada, Australia, New Zealand, and the Nordic countries. Many are under consideration for protection but they are also places with potential for fuel and mineral mining, forestry, hydropower and recreation. The development of indigenous energy supplies and the protection of wilderness may thus be in conflict.

----

1) U.S. Endangered Species Act of 1973.

Protection is given to some wildlife habitats and landscapes in many OECD countries and although there is no international definition for such areas, their extent appears to have increased in most countries between 1965 and 1975 with the establishment of public and private wildlife refuges and of national and regional parks (Table 11 and Annex 28). However, such habitats, even when protected by law or regulations, may be threatened by excessive visiting, accidental spills and construction plans.

Adverse effects on wildlife habitats can further be reduced by such means as better farming and forestry practices, better design of infrastructures, and more generally, by taking the protection of wildlife fully into account in relevant decisions.

Polluting Substances

Polluting substances affect the functioning of ecosystems of all kinds, even if present in only small amounts. Such pollutants originate from industrial processes, the use and disposal of consumer products and the application of fertilisers and pesticides. Water pollution affects plant growth and, of course, fish life in some countries. Acid precipitation may also affect forests. Some of the chemical pollutants, particularly the organochlorine compounds, persist in nature and are soluble in the tissues of minute organisms. As smaller organisms are consumed by larger ones, the amount of chemicals can build up until its presence is sufficient to affect these larger organisms. Large bird and mammal predators at the top of the food chain are most at risk. DDT, for example, may be found in zooplankton at concentrations of .04 parts per million, in needle fish at 2.0 parts per million and in cormorants, ospreys and other large fish-eating birds at 25 parts per million, a level high enough to affect reproduction. The accumulation of DDT in this way has been largely responsible for reproductive failure and poisoning of the bald eagle, the brown pelican and the peregrine falcon - all endangered species.

The potential of toxic substances present in the natural environment to affect wildlife and human health adversely was brought to the attention of the public in the 1960s. DDT and its derivatives were identified as primary suspects; other pesticides to attract concern were aldrin/dieldrin and lindane. The heavy metals such as mercury and lead also came under suspicion. Action was taken in many OECD countries to reduce the amount of DDT and its derivatives going into the environment in the early 1970s. OECD programmes of sampling and analysis of wildlife for environmental contaminants were also undertaken.

Recent results of these programmes show significant declines in concentrations of some of the more common organochlorines and mercury in samples of wildlife taken from marine, freshwater, and terrestrial environments (Figure 18). Residues of the DDT group (DDT, DDE, TDE) were found to have declined in 50 to 70 per cent of the samples examined. Residues of PCB's were found to be declining in 37 per cent and increasing in 14 per cent of the samples. Residues of mercury were found to have decreased in 55 per cent and to have increased in 18 per cent of the samples.(1)

In addition to these favourable findings, isolated increases in fledglings have been counted in some countries that have been attributed to reduced levels of toxic substances. More monitoring and analysis of additional substances will establish whether these findings will hold over longer periods. If they do, it will mean that controls on the use of at least some pesticides and other toxic substances and can effectively reduce their adverse effects on wildlife.

Some endangered species of wildlife have thus been protected by actions tailored to operate in certain places or against specific pollutants. Work is now developing on making broader concerns for wildlife an integral part of resource management, and on balancing ecological and biological concerns with economic demands for the use of these resources.

1) OECD (1979) "Programmes of wildlife sampling and analysis for environmental contaminants", forthcoming.

Figure 18

ENVIRONMENTAL CONTAMINANTS[a] IN WILDLIFE SAMPLES, OECD COUNTRIES
1972-1975

Contaminants	Number of Analyses	Trends		
		No Trends	Decreasing	Increasing
DDE	37	14	19	4
PCBs	35	17	13	5
Mercury	27	7	15	5

SAMPLING AREAS IN OECD COUNTRIES, 1972-1975 :

* Marine Environment
* Freshwater Environment
○ Terrestrial Environment

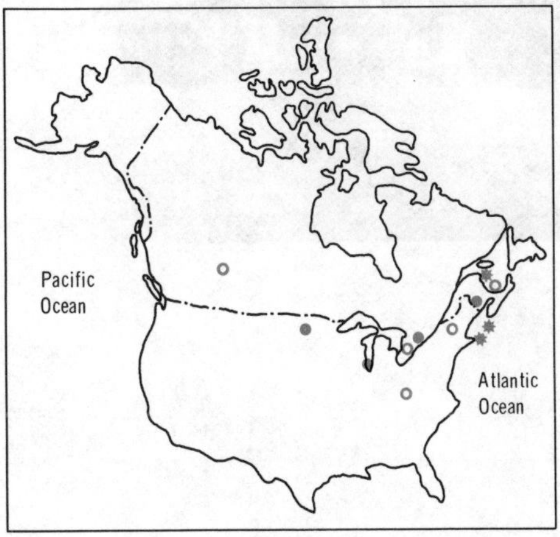

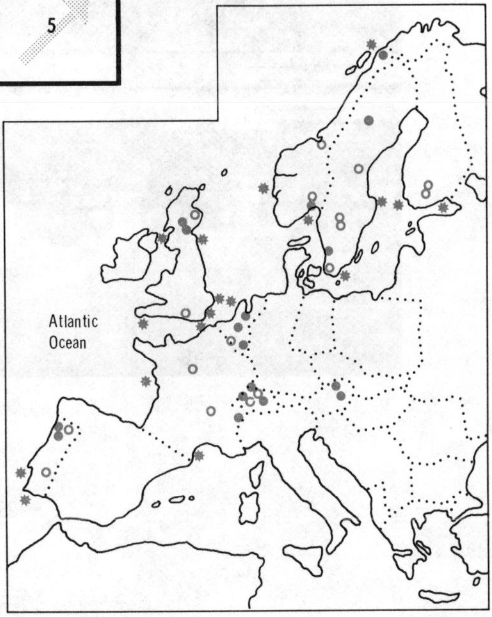

a) Results of the OECD programme on "Wildlife sampling and analysis for environmental contaminants" based on 66 samples of wildlife samples in freshwater, terrestrial and marine environments in OECD countries.

For details see Annex 29.

Chapter 5

CHEMICAL SUBSTANCES

More than four million different chemicals including natural
and man-made substances have been identified to date. Although most
of them have no commercial value, at least 60,000 are used in practical applications. Chemicals are made for a wide variety of industrial, agricultural, forestry, household, medical, cosmetic and
other purposes and both the number in commercial use and the volumes
produced have increased considerably in the last decade. Indeed,
the production of over 100 chemicals currently exceeds 50,000 tons
per year.

Chemicals find their way into the air, the water and the soil
in the course of their production, transport, use, or disposal. They
also enter the environment through various chemical reactions associated with the burning of fuel for power generation, for use in
motor vehicles and domestic heating. Some chemicals enter the environment as a result of direct application. These are mainly fertilizers, pesticides and herbicides.

Resolutions passed by the World Health Assembly in 1977 and 1978
indicate growing worldwide concern about the adverse effects of
chemicals on health.(1) These resolutions voiced special concern
about the risk of chronic or combined toxic effects from exposure
to chemicals. The increasing number of accidental releases of chemicals which have resulted in harm to man and the environment also
provided grounds for concern.

A better understanding of the potential hazards of chemicals to
health requires a knowledge of their pathways through ecosystems and
their transformation into different substances as well as their final
destination. Present knowledge with respect to these questions, however, is inadequate. For example, while it is natural that chemical
substances should be concentrated where they have been released,
their subsequent progress may depend on their degradability and their
ability to react with other substances as well as many other factors.
In some cases the new substances that result from chemical interaction are more hazardous than their parents. Different compounds

1) Resolutions WHA 30.47 and WHA 31.28.

Figure 19

SOURCES OF LEAD IN THE ECOSYSTEMS AND PATHWAYS OF LEAD TO MAN

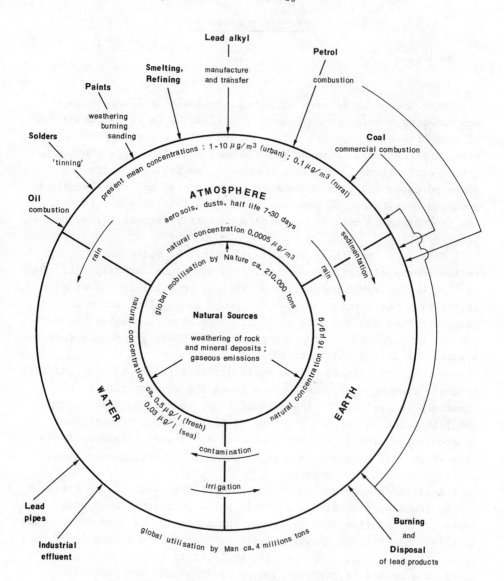

SOURCES OF LEAD IN THE ECOSYSTEM[a]

a) «Natural concentration» refer to pre-industrial levels of lead concentration ; «present urban concentrations» for atmosphere refers to average situations in industrialised countries.

Source : Department of the Environment (1974) "Lead in the environment and its significance to man", London, HMSO.

Figure 19 (contd.)

SOURCES OF LEAD IN THE ECOSYSTEMS AND PATHWAYS OF LEAD TO MAN

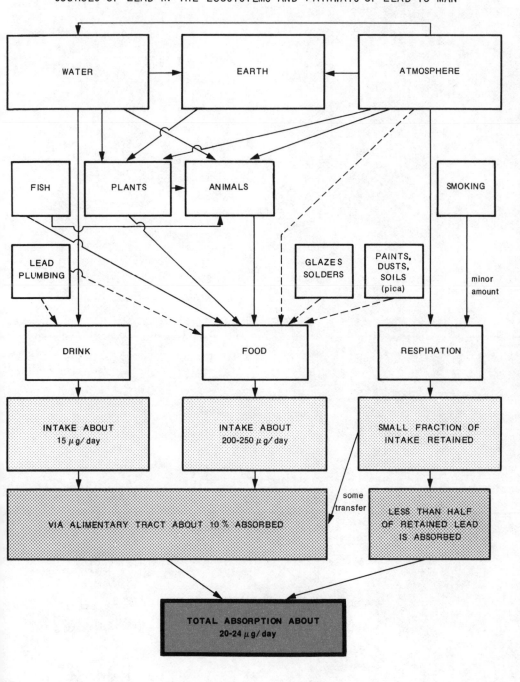

PATHWAYS OF LEAD TO MAN [a]

a) Pecked lines indicates exceptional source.

Source : Department of the Environment (1974) "Lead in the environment and its significance to man", London, HMSO.

may become transformed into identical intermediate or end products. The origin of certain substances found in the environment can therefore be difficult to trace. Some attempts have been made to chart the flow of certain chemicals or groups of chemicals through the environment. Lead, for example, has been traced in the United Kingdom and the resulting diagrams show the multiple sources of the metal as well as the different paths by which it reaches man (Figure 19).

Some chemicals do not break down readily or do so only partially. The problems that they can cause have been highlighted in an OECD study which has contributed significantly to the orientation of the work of the OECD Chemicals Group. The study indicates that in considering the impact of persistent chemicals the following characteristics are important: persistence in a biologically active form for prolonged periods under natural conditions; distribution at low concentrations in water and air, even if they are of only low solubility in water or of low volatility; tendency to accumulate in organisms which may only be exposed to low concentrations and where they can build up to biologically significant levels.[1] Examples of persistent chemicals are organochlorine compounds like DDT and aldrin, polychlorinated biphenyls (PCBs) and compounds of heavy metals.

An example of the accumulation of a persistent substance is provided in the history of the "Minamata" disease in Japan.[2] A chemical firm using an inorganic mercury catalyst in production, emitted mercury waste into Minamata Bay. The waste included the highly toxic methyl mercuric chloride, which accumulated in fish and other forms of marine life. Regular consumption of fish caught in the bay led to the poisoning of more than 1,500 people and caused 241 deaths. While the chemical plant has been in production since 1932 the disease was not identified until 1956 and although the toxic discharges were halted in 1960, their effects are still being registered.

Food is, of course, one of the basic pathways by which chemicals reach man and, as shown by the Minamata case, the effects can be serious if not lethal. However the risks to man due to the accumulation of chemicals in food are not sufficiently understood. Many food products contain small amounts of chemical additives to improve the flavour, colour and consistency, that may be absorbed and accumulated in the body over long periods. Crops treated with pesticides and herbicides usually also contain at least trace amounts of the chemicals used. Meat, dairy and poultry products may

1) OECD (1971), "The Problems of Persistent Chemicals", Paris.
2) OECD (1977), "Mercury and Environment", Paris.

contain traces of antibiotics, hormones and other chemicals that have been added to animal feed. Tin, plastics and other packaging materials can give off chemical residues. Work on evaluating food additives, assessing levels of residues, and establishing acceptable daily intakes is now under way, mainly under the auspices of the Food and Agricultural Organisation and the World Health Organisation and provides guidelines for decision-making. Many uncertainties remain about the effects of chemicals on health, however. The possibility that some chemicals may exhibit side-effects which affect genetic development cannot be excluded. Progress in this field is handicapped by a lack of knowledge about how and why certain chemicals augment or weaken the effects of others.

The study of hazardous substances was focused at first upon single doses of chemicals which caused death or serious harm to people. Current attention is focused on such longer term effects of exposure to different doses of chemicals as genetic mutations, and birth deformities. A number of chemicals cause, or are suspected to cause, cancer. Clinical observations, epidemiological surveys and experiments all support this conclusion though many uncertainties surround it. Compared with the total number of chemicals used, only a few have been studied to see whether they cause cancer mainly because of the high cost of tests of this kind. Yet there is increasing evidence that substances such as vinyl chloride can produce cancer. Evidence of related undesirable effects from other chemicals may be expected but may become clear only later because of the long delay between exposure to a carcinogen and the occurrence of disease. In general, the latency period may extend for as long as 15 to 20 years. Cancers caused by chemicals usually result from direct exposure to certain substances. However, other mechanisms exist. It is currently suspected that chlorofluorocarbons may indirectly contribute to skin cancer.

The harmful effects of many chemicals have been confirmed through the study of the relationship between working conditions and health. Diseases due to asbestos and chromates are notable examples.

The consequences of increasing use of chemicals are complex. No doubt much of the technology and wealth of modern society could not have been developed without progress in the field of chemicals. Yet chemicals have brought with them new hazards to man and his environment. Attempts have been made to create a systematic basis for evaluating these risks and benefits but the results have so far been limited. One difficulty is that the benefits often accrue to one group while the risks are incurred by another. A further difficulty is how to translate damage to health and the environment into monetary values, especially where the damage can be irreversible.

The effects on people of exposure to chemicals may be studied in various ways. One is to examine the long term effects on the community as a whole. However increasing importance is being placed upon improved and extended study of people who, because of their jobs, are subject to additional exposure to chemicals. Children, pregnant women, the elderly and other groups are also particularly sensitive.

In 1973 the OECD Council made a decision about the control of polychlorinated biphenyls (PCBs).(1) Later in the same year the Council recommended measures to reduce all man-made emissions of mercury.(2) In order to follow the results of these actions in Member countries, statistics on the production, use and disposal of PCBs and mercury were collected from 1973 through 1976. Analysis of the results shows a progressive decrease in the production of PCBs (Table 15) but also that the existing data, which are mainly kept for trade purposes, do not always satisfy needs for environmental purposes. One reason is that chemicals used as components of products are not necessarily declared. Another is that chemicals may be grouped in a way that prevents the identification of compounds of special interest from an environmental viewpoint.

To summarise, chemicals can generate hazards and can damage man and his environment. The magnitude of the problems and the mechanisms involved have been the subject of increasing study over the past 10-15 years, but much remains unknown. Methods for making assessments and judgments in this particularly complex field are imperfect and how to extrapolate to man evidence gained from the study of animals is a basic problem. However action has been taken in most Member countries to restrict or ban the use of selected persistent chemicals such as DDT, aldrin, dieldrin, PCBs and alkyl-mercury compounds. Further action of this kind may be expected as better information on chemicals becomes available.

The need to scrutinise new chemicals before marketing is increasingly recognised and this represents the thinking behind some legislation recently enacted or planned in Member countries. The main objective is to assess in advance the risks associated with a chemical and to regulate its use, if appropriate, before rather than after damage has occurred. This is also the philosophy of an OECD Council Recommendation of 1977 establishing guidelines for anticipating the effects of chemicals.(3) The chemicals testing programme

1) OECD (1973), Decision of the Council "On Protection of the Environment by Control of Polychlorinated Biphenyls", Paris.

2) OECD (1973), "Recommendation of the Council on Measures to Reduce All Man-Made Emissions of Mercury to the Environment", Paris.

3) OECD (1977), "Recommendation of the Council Establishing Guidelines in Respect of Procedure and Requirements for Anticipating the Effects of Chemicals on Man and in the Environment", Paris.

at OECD is a joint effort by Member countries to implement the
Recommendation and the recently started special programme on the
control of chemicals is an additional move to improve the basis
for action and to achieve international harmonization.(1) Its objectives are to make more efficient use of resources and to control
chemicals so as to protect man's health and environment.

1) OECD (1978), "Decision of the Council Concerning a Special Programme on the Control of Chemicals", Paris.

Table 15. PRODUCTION[a] OF POLYCHLORINATED BIPHENYLS (PCBs), OECD COUNTRIES, 1973-1977

(tons)

COUNTRY	1973	1974	1975	1976	1977
France	9,674	9,541	7,182	7,190	..
Germany	6,949	8,374	7,328	6,610	5,680
Italy	2,519	..	1,868	1,933	..
Spain	..	2,386	..	..	1,504
United Kingdom .	4,067	4,818	3,274	3,013	283
USA	19,132	18,394	14,207	13,423	6,046
OECD Total[b] ...	42,341	43,513	33,859	32,169	13,513

NOTES:

a)   Data as of February 1979.

b)   The table covers all PCBs producing countries in OECD; totals are however incomplete.

Chapter 6

NOISE

Noise comprises unwanted or excessive sounds. It may be defined more precisely as any sound that can produce undesired physiological and psychological effects on individuals or groups. It
is measured in decibels.(1)

In daily life, one is generally exposed to noise fluctuating
from between 30 and 40 decibels to between 80 and 90 decibels or
even more. Various indices have been developed for assessing the
impacts of noise and for regulating exposure to it, but there is a
strong trend in most countries toward the use of the L_{eq} "equivalent
sound level", a scale that can be used for assessing the noise impact
from most sources. Data concerning noise exposure will therefore be
expressed in L_{eq} in this chapter.

1. Effects of exposure to noise

Exposure to noise is of concern for the quality of life in
general because of (i) its effects on health, (ii) its effects on
behaviour and activities, (iii) its psychological and social
effects.(2)

The hearing of an individual will not be impaired if the daily
equivalent sound level in his environment is no more than 70 decibels
over a lifetime and no more than an L_{eq} of 75 decibels during eight

---

1) The noise emitted is only a tiny fraction (approximately one-
millionth) of the mechanical energy essentially expended by industrial and urban activities.

A decibel (dB) is a unit of measure of sound pressure level related to a standard reference level of 0.00002 Newtons per square
metre. The decibel scale is logarithmic so that a very wide range
of audible sound can be described in terms of a manageably small
range of numerical expressions. A sound of 0 dB at 1000 hertz
would be just audible to a person with good hearing. A sound of
120 dB would cause pain in the ear. The acoustical pressure of
the second is one million times greater than that of the first.

A decibel A-weighted (dBA) is a unit of measure of sound in which
greater emphasis is given to medium and high frequencies to which
the human ear is most sensitive. The dBA measure, which is the
most usual in noise abatement and control activities, gives a good
correlation with the subjective impression of loudness.

A 10 decibels increase of the sound doubles the subjective intensity of that sound (i.e. its loudness or noisiness), whereas a
doubling of the acoustic energy results only in an increase of
3 decibels.

2) OECD (1978), "Reducing Noise in OECD Countries", Paris.

hours per day.(1) In several European countries the safety level
adopted to prevent permanent hearing loss is a daily equivalent sound
level of no more than 80 decibels (A). It should be noted that permanent hearing impairment is generally associated with occupational
noise rather than with daily environmental noise except in the cases
of prolonged exposure to high noise levels (e.g. people living near
a source of loud noise or drivers of very noisy vehicles, including
recreational vehicles). In many countries, hearing damage due to
occupational noise is now considered an illness subject to
compensation.

Besides temporary or permanent damage to hearing, noise causes
stress by triggering automatic and unconscious physiological reactions, including higher blood pressure, faster heart beat and breathing, and a higher rate of release of hormones into the blood.
People may be desensitised to noise, although some biological responses still occur. Noise may also contribute to heart and circula-
tory disease, and it may cumulate with other stresses.(2)

Obviously, noise can affect both the period and the quality of
sleep and certain people, notably the elderly and the sick, are more
sensitive to disruptive noise. Work efficiency and well-being during
daytime may also suffer if sleep is disrupted.

Besides sleep, conversation and listening to TV and radio are
among the activities which are most frequently disturbed by noise.
The interference of noise with communication increases rapidly
above 50 dBA. For good perception when listening to radio or television, noise should not exceed 45 dBA.(3)

It has been argued that noise may also hinder the development
of language skills in children and disrupt their education.(2)

The most obvious effect of environmental noise is simple annoyance. Yet, such is the complexity of subjective reactions, that
the degree and level of individual annoyance cannot be predicted.
Nonetheless, it is possible to relate in statistical terms the percentage of people in a certain location who are "highly annoyed" and
the level of outdoor noise of that location. The most recent studies
indicate that the relationship between noise exposure and the percentage of highly annoyed people is exponential; almost no one is

---

1) Commission of the European Communities (1975), "Damage and
   Annoyance Caused by Noise", Luxembourg.

   US-EPA (1974), "Information on Levels of Environmental Noise
   Requisite to Protect Public Health and Welfare with an Adequate
   Margin of Safety".

2) US-EPA (1978), "Noise: a Health Problem".

3) Commission of the European Communities (1975), "Damage and Annoyance caused by Noise", Luxembourg.

annoyed below an outdoor L_{eq} of 45 dBA, almost 10 per cent of the people are annoyed at an L_{eq} of 55 dBA and everybody is annoyed at an L_{eq} of 85 dBA. Between these two limits, the percentage of "highly annoyed" persons roughly doubles for every increase of 10 decibels.(1)

High noise levels may result in formal complaints to authorities sometimes culminating in community action or litigation. However, complaints are not necessarily considered a reliable guide to the significance of noise problems, mainly because social and political factors may influence the "representativeness" of the remonstration.

2. The state of noise

The extent of noise

Over the past 15 years or so noise has been extended in time (night traffic, weekend and holiday activities) and in space (noise in residential suburbs). The total noise energy output doubled over the same period in OECD Member countries. These changes are closely related to densities of population and activities and to the growing use of motor vehicles for the movement of people and goods.(2) In the United States, for instance, both traffic noise and aircraft noise have increased continuously since 1950 and, in the decade up to 1970, "noise impacted land" lying within an L_{eq} contour of 65 dBA has in fact risen by a factor of 7 near airports and freeways.(3) In Osaka in Japan a survey showed that between 1955 and 1968, daytime noise levels increased only slightly in the city centre but substantially by 15 dBA in residential areas at night.(4)

Emissions of Noise

The dominant source of noise in the daily outdoor environment is transport especially motor vehicles and aircraft. But noise from fixed sources (factories, workshops, and various miscellaneous sources), due to construction activities (construction of buildings and other infrastructure) and to some leisure activities also leads to annoyance. Heavy trucks and noisy first generation jet aircraft produce over half of all noise energy and are responsible for the main part of the annoyance caused from noise.

1) Schultz, T.J. (1978), "Social Surveys on Noise Annoyance", 3rd International Congress on Noise as a Public Health Problem, Freiburg, Germany.
2) OECD (1978), "Reducing Noise in OECD Countries".
3) Calculations derived from the "Report to the President and Congress on Noise", Washington, United States, 1972.
4) "Environmental Pollution in Osaka Prefecture", Japan (1970).

Exposure of people to noise

Although the importance of occupational noise is recognised, this discussion focuses on exposure of people to noise from road traffic and air traffic for two reasons. First, very little information exists for estimating the number of people affected by noise from such sources as industry and construction. The same is true of noise from lawnmowers and household appliances. Second, as stated by the OECD Ad Hoc Group on Noise Abatement Polices, "the source of noise which disturbs the largest number of people for the longest periods is transport"[1] Table 16 shows the percentages of the population of various OECD countries exposed to given noise levels.

It would appear that between 10 and 20 per cent of the population in OECD countries live in areas exposed to outdoor noise levels in excess of 65 dBA (daily L_{eq} or L_{eq} 24 hours). 65 dBA is considered as an upper limit of "tolerance" or "acceptability"[2], and in several countries, this level serves as a basis for the regulation of compensation and for noise insulation. The margin of error in these figures is large since the data are generally estimates based on population density and traffic volumes rather than on comprehensive measurements. Noise problems from road traffic are, not surprisingly, concentrated in urban areas and traffic levels tend to vary in parallel with population density.[3] Large conurbations, therefore, usually experience higher noise levels than medium and smaller towns. For instance, two recent surveys showed that average outdoor noise levels in London and Paris are about 7 dBA above the averages in other conurbations.[3][4] In a city like Paris, nearly half of the population is living in areas exposed to outdoor noise levels exceeding an L_{eq} of 65 dBA.[4]

A comparison of aircraft and traffic noise figures shows that aircraft noise disturbs fewer people than traffic noise even though the former is a much more important source of annoyance than the latter for residents close to airports. Figures also show that the loudest aircraft noise is greater than the loudest traffic noise. In the United States, aircraft noise affects (i.e. creates an exposure to more than a daily L_{eq} of 65 dBA) three to four times fewer people than traffic noise. In Europe or Japan some 20 times fewer people are affected by aircraft noise than by traffic noise. This

1) OECD (1978), "Reducing Noise in OECD Countries", Paris.
2) French "Ministère de l'Equipement" (1976), "Guide du bruit des transports terrestres", Paris.
3) United Kingdom Department of the Environment and Department of Transport (1977) "Noise and Road Traffic Outside Homes in England", London.
4) Institut de Recherche des Transports (1978), "Enquête nationale sur l'exposition des Français aux nuisances des transports", Lyon, France.

Table 16. POPULATION EXPOSED TO AIRCRAFT AND ROAD TRAFFIC NOISE, SELECTED COUNTRIES OR REGIONS, mid-1970s (per cent)

AIRCRAFT NOISE % of national population exposed to given levels (a) (b)				NOISE LEVEL in Leq (dBA) outdoor measures		ROAD TRAFFIC NOISE % of national population exposed to given noise levels (b)											
United States (c)	Canada (d)	Japan (c)	Europe (e)			United States (a)	Japan (f)	Belgium (f)	Denmark (f)	France (f)	Germany (f)	Netherlands (f)	Norway (a)	Spain (f)	Sweden (a)	Switzerland (f)	United Kingdom (g)
13	2	3	3	≥ 55	Sleep can be disturbed if windows are open	40	80	68	50	47	72	..	22	74	41.5	66	50
5	1	1	1	≥ 60	Sleep and conversation can be disturbed if windows are open	18	58	39	..	32	46	30	12	50	25	28	27
2	1	0.5	0.2	≥ 65	Sleep and conversation can be disturbed even if windows are closed	6.4	31	12	20	14	18	7.4	5	23	12.5	12	11
0.6	0.3	0.2	0.05	≥ 70	Sleep and conversation disturbance; possible complaints	1.8	10	1	..	4	4	1.6	2	7	..	1	4
0.2	0.1	0.1	0.01	≥ 75	Possible long-term danger for hearing ability	—	1	—	..	0.5	—	0.1	—	1	..	—	1

(a) Expressed in Leq over 24 hours.
(b) Data refers to various years in the early Seventies for different countries. Since many measurements and surveys do not give results in Leq, equations relating Leq and other indices have been used. The margin of error due to national estimates, different years, and to this transformation are probably very important, especially at lower level of noise (±10%).
(c) For all airports.
(d) For 5 major airports (Edmunton, Montreal, Ottawa, Toronto, Vancouver).
(e) For 34 airports. Broad assumptions were made concerning densities around some airports.
(f) Expressed in Leq over the period 6-22 h.
(g) Expressed in Leq over the period 6-24 h, England only.

suggests that aircraft noise is relatively more important in the United States than in Europe and that conversely, traffic noise is relatively more important in Europe which has a higher density of vehicles, narrower streets, and vehicles with engines running at higher speed than in the United States.

3. The future of noise

Forecasts made in some countries suggest that, in spite of existing regulations and actions taken to reduce noise, the number of people exposed to high levels of noise will increase. In the United Kingdom, for instance, the number of city dwellers exposed to traffic noise levels higher than about L_{eq} 67 dBA is expected to increase by 600,000 between 1975 and 1985;(1) in France, the number of people exposed to more than L_{eq} 66 dBA is expected to increase by 800,000 between now and 1985 if the noise emitted by new motor vehicles is not reduced. In the United States, a three to fourfold increase is projected in the number of residents adjacent to freeways and major highways who will be exposed to "high noise levels" (exceeding an L_{eq} of 62 dBA) by the year 2000.(2) Such increases are expected to be mainly due to increases in traffic volumes and to continued urban sprawl.

Noise is thus expected to spread outside currently busy areas, especially to the suburbs and, perhaps even more important, to tourist and wilderness areas such as mountains and coastal areas during weekends and holidays. This is because leisure activities and tourism continue to increase and also because more secondary homes are being built.(3) The impact of noise around airports should evolve as the fleet of noisy aircraft is replaced by quieter ones. However, aviation may be expected to increase rapidly and noise will become an increasing problem around numerous airports which are as yet not very busy but which may become so.

Today noise is the problem ranked highest by people(4) in numerous surveys concerning the undesirable aspects of living conditions. It is also a problem that can be expected to persist and grow unless strong and effective noise abatement policies are adopted.

---

1) OECD (1978) "Reducing Noise in OECD Countries".
2) US-EPA (1977) "Toward a Strategy for Noise Control".
3) Institut de Recherche des Transports (1975) "Exposition des Français au bruit et à la pollution due à la circulation automobile", Lyon.
4) US-EPA (1977) "Toward a national strategy for noise control", Washington, D.C.

Part Three

THE RESPONSES

Alleviation of Stresses on the Environment

PART THREE

THE RESPONSES

The way in which the growth of man's activities has placed added
pressures on the environment and the state of the environment itself
are outlined in earlier parts of this report. It is now time to turn
to man's responses to the challenges presented by his own dynamism.
Many people have been and are involved. Consumers, industrialists,
administrators, scientists, politicians, journalists and many others
have all played a part in combatting environmental pollution. Some
people have even changed their behaviour. Despite the difficulties
involved, the challenge has been met with noteworthy speed and
effectiveness. Problems have been analysed, action taken and results
achieved. It is no exaggeration to say that many other pressing
issues are being handled less successfully.

The anatomy of this response has differed in detail from country
to country but it has often followed similar patterns. The public
at large, often led by activists and helped by the media, has started
things off by demanding environmental improvements. This, in turn,
has led Governments to pass laws and to create institutions designed
to control pollution, manage resources and improve the amenity of
towns and the country. Finally, industry has taken steps to reduce
pollution and conserve resources. Although this over-simplifies the
complex interaction of the different respondents, it does illustrate
the response of the major groups with which this part of the report
is concerned.

The Public

Concern about the environment is not unique to our time. It
has foundations that date at least from the first great wave of
industrialisation when enlightened individuals campaigned for sani-
tary reform in cities and industrialists built model mills and houses
for their workers. The concern, however, about what was happening
to air, water, landscape and other natural resources that emerged
in most Member countries in the late 1960s was new in its scope and
depth. It was not restricted to a few philanthropists or specialists.
For the first time it was felt and voiced by large numbers of people

121

from many walks of life. Wide scale public reaction followed. In Japan, for instance, complaints about environmental degradation, which were hardly heard at all in 1960, increased to about 20,000 by 1966, reached a peak of some 80,000 in 1972, and stabilized at about 70,000 in 1974. In Europe, the Commission of the European Communities identified more than 20,000 associations for the protection of the environment in 1975 and considered the estimate a low one.

The activities of the public were manifold and moves were taken against polluters by individuals as well as by groups. They ranged from legal actions in the courts to violent demonstrations in the streets. In some countries, such as France, Germany and New Zealand, "ecological" candidates stood for office at national, regional or municipal elections. In 1972 the United Nations Conference in Stockholm both reflected and re-inforced the development of this awareness.

Several explanations can be offered for this widespread surge of interest in the environment. First, it can be related to a deterioration in the environment, which, if not now measurable, was widely perceived to have taken place after 1945. During this period degradation was thought to have changed in nature, and probably in magnitude; undoubtedly it became more obvious. This view was re-inforced by a large number of books, reports and studies that received wide circulation, as well as the exposure given to severe pollution episodes and accidents by the media.

A second explanation reflects the assumption that a good environment becomes increasingly important to people as their incomes rise. It is, therefore, argued that the rapid rise in incomes that took place in the sixties and early seventies quite naturally brought about an even greater increase in the demand for clean air, clean beaches and unspoilt country. It was all part of a demand for a better quality of life.

A third explanation can be found in the linkage that was inferred in the late sixties between economic growth and pollution. As continued growth was expected, pollution could be - and was - forecast to increase at the same rate. This focussed attention not so much on current conditions as on those that could be expected in the future, especially if no action or inadequate action was taken. Many people believed that pollution was eluding man's control. This view was no doubt strengthened by space shots of planet earth with its finite biosphere that sustains complex ecosystems of which man was clearly an integral part. In addition, the notion of ecological limits to growth coupled with finite natural resources had a profound public impact.

122

For these and many other reasons the demand for environmental quality secured a strong and enduring influence on national policy. The strength of this demand has been undiminished by the economic stagnation of recent years. In 1976, people in the countries of the European Communities were asked to rank the importance of topical issues. On average they placed the protection of the environment third after fighting unemployment and inflation (Annex 30). In Denmark, France, Luxembourg and the Netherlands environment was placed second. Other surveys in the United States and Japan pointed in 1976 in a similar direction. In the United States, for example 67 per cent of the public thought water pollution to be "very serious". These levels of concern were significantly greater than they had been in 1973 before the economic recession. Asked about environmental problems 70 per cent of respondents in the United States and 80 per cent in Japan (excluding don't knows) saw them as a "serious threat" (Annex 31).

Other more recent surveys go further and indicate what people say they are willing to pay for environmental quality. Thus when Americans, Canadians and Japanese were asked whether they would rather pay more to protect the environment, or pay lower prices, but have more air and water pollution, 62 per cent in the United States (in 1978), 57 per cent in Canada (in 1978) and 72 per cent in Japan (in 1975) said that they would choose to pay more. Equally significant is the finding that concern for a good environment and willingness to pay for it is present in various income groups in North America.

Increasingly, these demands for improved environmental quality are being taken into account by policy makers. A number of mechanisms are being developed in Member countries to cope with this new and often difficult task. They are of three main kinds.

First, there are mechanisms aimed at the collection of information on what the public wants. These include household surveys, complaints boxes, public hearings on specific projects and links with associations of consumers and environmentalists, including groups such as anglers, who depend on natural resources for their sport or recreation. Public inquiry procedures may also be used to enable interested individuals and groups to make their views known before decisions are taken on developments. In the United Kingdom an elaborate inquiry of this kind was recently held on proposals for a nuclear waste treatment plant at Windscale. All such techniques help to inform policy makers of people's wants and are increasingly used in many countries.

Second, there are mechanisms for involving the public in the planning process. Some, such as giving representatives of associations seats on planning and consultative bodies, provide for regular interaction. Others such as environmental impact assessments offer once-and-for-all chances to groups and, in some cases, individuals to voice concerns about, and to suggest modifications or alternatives to, particular projects.

Finally, there are mechanisms that provide the interested public with a role in decision-making. In France, for instance, representatives of recognised associations sit on boards charged with managing river basins, and on agencies concerned with national parks, the conservation of open land around Paris, coastal protection and the disposal of industrial waste. In the United States and Switzerland referenda on projects affecting the environment are sometimes organised at state or local levels and their results can be binding. In Sweden citizens can bring certain types of environmental cases before a National Board which acts as a court.

The orderly development and use of such mechanisms is not easy and raises questions not all of which have been answered. In some cases access to the courts is not available by right to environmental associations; in others procedures for taking decisions do not allow the public to be involved. However, where opportunities for participation exist, they make it possible for the public to express demands for environmental quality in an orderly and constructive manner. Experience suggests that demands would not be reduced if no such channels were available, that they might be exacerbated, and would probably be voiced in less efficient ways.

Information not only flows from citizens to their governments; it also flows back in the form of publications, educational television and exhibitions. Periodic state of the environment reports published by national governments and policy studies such as those produced by OECD on Sweden and Japan illustrate other official efforts to provide the public with useful environmental information.

Public Decision Makers

Governments and other public bodies were amongst those who reacted to the environmental challenge of the 1960s. This does not mean they had done nothing earlier. In many countries national parks and environmental protection policies had long been established. However, in the late sixties and in the early seventies, and in practically all countries, general and specialised environmental laws were passed (Table 17) and institutions set up to implement them.

Table 17. MAJOR NATIONAL ENVIRONMENTAL LAWS (a), OECD COUNTRIES
1956-1968/1969-1979

Country \ Type of Law	General	Water	Wastes	Air	Impact Statement	Other
Canada		1970			1973	1975 (b)
United States		1972 1977	1965 1970 1976	1963 1970 1977	1969	1976 (b)
Japan	1967 1970	1958 1970	1970	1962 1968		1973 (b) 1974 (c)
Australia	1974				1974	
New Zealand		1967 1974		1972	1972 1977	
Austria		1959				1973
Belgium		1971	1974	1964		
Denmark	1973		1976			
Finland		1961 1965	1978			1965 (d)
France	1976	1964	1975	1974	1976	1977 (b)
Germany		1957 1976	1972	1974	1975	1976 (g)
Greece	1976	1978				
Iceland						
Ireland	1976	1977		1977	1976	
Italy		1976		1966		
Luxembourg	..	..	..	..	1978	..
Netherlands		1970 1975	1976 1977	1972		1979 (e)
Norway		1970				1977 (b)
Portugal	1976					
Spain			1975	1972		
Sweden	1969	1969	1975	1969	(1969) (f)	1964 (g) 1973 (b)
Switzerland		1971				1969 (b)
Turkey		1971				
United Kingdom	1974	1961 1974	1972	1956		1975 (c)

(a) Some federal countries such as Australia and Austria have laws at state level.
(b) Law on the general control of chemicals.
(c) Law on compensation.
(d) Law on public health.
(e) Law on noise.
(f) Essentially a specific administrative procedure.
(g) Law on nature conservancy.

In some countries, the environmental responsibilities of existing ministries were enlarged. This is the case for instance with
the Ministry of Agriculture in Sweden, the Ministry of Health in the
Netherlands, and the Ministries of the Interior in Germany and
Finland. In other countries such as the United Kingdom and, since
1978, France, larger ministries, also responsible for housing and
urban affairs, were formed. In yet other countries such as the
United States, Japan, Norway, Canada and, until 1978, France more
specialised Environment Ministries were created. In some cases,
states, provinces or regions, and cities also created agencies that
are often as important and as influential as their national counter-
parts. In Japan, the number of officials in charge of pollution
abatement in the prefectures and cities is about twelve times greater
than in central government.

Environmental objectives were also defined. Some objectives
took the form of quality or ambient standards, setting out maximum
permissible levels of pollutants for bodies of air or water. Ambient
standards are usually, but not always, set by central governments.
In some countries they are complemented by limits to emissions that
define the amount of pollutants that may be discharged. Such limits
may relate to a specific body of water, such as a river basin, or to
the air above a metropolitan region, or even an entire country. This
is done, for instance, for air and water pollution in Japan and for
water pollution in France. As a rule ambient standards and total
emission limits are only guidelines or targets and do not, by themselves, impose specific constraints upon polluters. In Japan, however, area emission limits play an important role in the apparatus
of control and are used to impose constraints on polluters.

Objectives have also been set in many countries to conserve
natural resources and enhance amenities, particularly in and near
towns. Where the objective is to set up national parks and nature
reserves decisions are generally taken by central governments but
the creation of amenities, such as green belts and pedestrian streets
and the rehabilitation of derelict land, is more often done by local
authorities in the context of development plans. Growing importance
is attached in many Member countries to conserving land, as well as
other natural resources, and increasing their usefulness through
using them for several purposes.

Governments may pursue environmental objectives by direct or
indirect means. In the former case the spending of tax revenues by
public agencies will be involved. Indirect actions, on the other
hand, usually involve placing constraints on, or offering incentives
to, private bodies. They usually lead to private expenditure.

Direct action includes the disposal or treatment of solid or liquid wastes, the provision of parks and the laying out of recreation areas. Such actions are usually the responsibility of local authorities and they have become particularly important during the last decade. The number of people served by sewers has increased greatly, water treatment plants have multiplied, more sophisticated methods of refuse collection and disposal have appeared and many parks and recreation areas have been created or improved. Capital and current expenditure on such urban public services (though not a good indicator) accounted in recent years for between 1 and 4 per cent of gross domestic product in OECD countries. Examples of direct actions undertaken primarily by central government are research, data collection, reporting and information. Their development has also been very rapid in recent years.

Environmental policies are also implemented indirectly by placing constraints on polluters so as to eliminate, or better still, prevent pollution. Furthermore, the "polluter pays principle" adopted by the OECD in 1972, specifically states that such indirect action should not involve public funds except for the relatively small amounts required for planning, monitoring and enforcement.(1) This explains why budget appropriations should not be used to judge the scale of action of government in raising the quality of the environment.

The granting or withholding of authorisation is one of the three main types of indirect action available to governments to protect the environment and laws have been enacted in most countries to make such authorisation mandatory for certain potentially harmful activities. The authorisation procedures themselves, the types of activities controlled, and the public bodies empowered to grant permission, all vary from country to country. The certification of drugs and chemicals, the granting of building permits and, more generally, development control, are typical of actions that enable governments to say "no" to potentially harmful actions and, for instance, to prevent excessive building in such sensitive areas as sea coasts. An important aspect of this type of indirect action is that it acts as a deterrent as well as a filter. Its efficiency cannot therefore be measured by just counting refusals. The very existence of the procedure is bound to influence the nature of products or projects submitted for scrutiny.

---

1) "Guiding Principles concerning International Economic Aspects of Environmental Policies". Recommendation adopted by the OECD Council on 26th May, 1972.

"The Implementation of the Polluter Pays Principle". Recommendation adopted by the OECD Council on 14th November, 1974.

Environmental impact assessment mechanisms give added value to this type of action by improving the quality of evidence available to the authorities and in some cases the public. The use of such procedures is spreading in accordance with an OECD Recommendation.(1) One such mechanism, the environmental impact statement procedure, is in use in Canada, the United States, Australia, New Zealand, France, Germany and Sweden. Others are being introduced progressively in other countries such as Greece.

A recent initiative, with an international dimension, by the United States Government has made it mandatory for public agencies and private firms to use procedures of this kind when in receipt of Federal funds and when acting in any way that might affect "global concerns" such as the oceans, the Antartic, or the environment of another country. In such cases the agency or firm will be obliged to assess the environmental consequences of the proposed action and file an impact report, which may be made available to other nations as appropriate.

A second type of indirect government action is the setting of emission standards that specify the quantity of pollutants (or their concentration in effluents) that may be discharged from a given source over a given period. Standards that define the physical or chemical properties of a product or the maximum permissible emissions from a product during use can be placed in the same category. Practically all Member countries set emission standards and the responsibility for doing so can rest with central or local governments. In some countries such as Japan, the United Kingdom and France, standards are formally or informally negotiated for sectors of industry or at the level of firms and even individual plants. In Japan this can take the form of a limit to emissions from a specific plant.

A third type of indirect government action comprises the setting of pollution charges. In a number of cases such charges are in effect a tax assessed on the amount of pollutants discharged into the environment. Firms may choose to continue their discharges, but the more they do, the more they pay. If the rate of charge is set high enough, firms will clearly find it economical to spend this money on emission control and, thus, to abate their pollution. Pollution charges are often directly related to an authorisation to discharge residuals: even if the emission is permitted the firm must pay.

The design of constraints of this kind, like the design of emission standards, often requires data that are not available.(2)

1) "The Analysis of the Environmental Consequences of Significant Public and Private Projects". Recommendation adopted by the OECD Council on 14th November, 1974.

2) See OECD (1976) "Pollution Charges: An Assessment", Paris.

Table 18.   POLLUTION RELATED CHARGES[a]
AND TAXES, OECD COUNTRIES, 1979

TYPE OF POLLUTION			
WATER	SOLID WASTES	AIR	NOISE
Canada			
		Japan	Japan
Finland	Finland		
France			France
Germany	Germany		
Netherlands		Netherlands	Netherlands
	Norway	Norway	
	Sweden		
United Kingdom			

NOTES:
a)   The nature and importance of the charges vary greatly from country to country.

Charges and taxes are nevertheless in use in at least nine Member countries, even though the scope of some of them is limited (Table 18). The French noise charge, for instance, is a mere landing fee that does not induce air transport companies to reduce aircraft noise.

Pollution charges are not widely used even by those Member countries that have adopted them. In many cases they are used to raise revenue rather than to induce polluters to reduce their emissions. However, there is a growing interest in the use of charges and, more generally, in the use of the market mechanisms. The market is a system where information is transmitted by prices, not by directives, and where action is motivated by profit. When, as in the case of pollution, the market fails, the authorities may choose to intervene by modifying prices which, in this case, means charging for pollution, or they may choose to make regulations. In the past administrators have tended to prefer the second course because it seemed more practical. Some economists have argued, however, that pricing mechanisms could achieve a given objective at a lower cost than regulatory ones. In practice, the nature of government intervention is often determined by a variety of factors, of which economic efficiency is but one, and the three types of indirect actions are seldom used in isolation. In the majority of cases, indeed, it has been found that using them together - regulations and charges together, for instance - is most practicable and effective.

The International Community

Environmental issues do not respect national boundaries, and a need to deal with them at the international level has been recognised for a number of years. An early response of international organisations was to draw out ideas, information and experience about environmental protection and to assist in their exchange. In a relatively new field, where international channels of communications were in the making, this role proved to be important. Not only has it enabled Member countries to learn from the experience of one another, but it has also contributed to the harmonization of policy.

A second response concerned transfrontier pollution. Pollutants carried across borders by water or air can contaminate the rivers, lakes, seas and the atmosphere of the "receiving" country. Experience shows that success in abating transfrontier pollution depends on efforts in both the countries where the pollution originates and where it is received, and thus on international collaboration.

Typically the collection and assessment of information about the sources and their effects is a necessary first step. After that different abatement strategies and their costs may be examined. One example of this was a study by the OECD of the long-range transport of sulphur dioxide over Europe. It was designed to identify the geographical origins of the pollutants received by a group of countries. In another case, the Rhine, data on emissions and concentrations of pollutants were collected by the International Commission, which then examined various ways of reducing pollution in the river.

The solution of transfrontier pollution problems is often extremely difficult, but it can be facilitated by the definition and acceptance of certain principles. Sets of guidelines developed by the OECD illustrate this approach. One principle, for example, concerns non-discrimination by one state against the citizens of another. This necessitates treating the citizens of a neighbouring country as the equals of those in the home country and treating the environment as if frontiers did not exist. The second principle concerns the notification of potentially affected countries by a government that certain actions are proposed by it and that consultation will be undertaken with authorities in affected countries if they request it. The objective is to get the facts out in the open, preferably before the event, and to facilitate negotiations.

In particular situations international guidelines in the form of emission or quality standards or regulations prohibiting noxious discharges such as mercury or untreated sewage, can be established. This was done in the Oslo, Paris, London, Helsinki and Barcelona conventions on marine pollution. It has also been done in connection with international rivers and lakes such as the Rhine, Lake Constance and Lake Leman.

Specialised international bodies may also be set up to deal with environmental problems. Often called "international commissions", they may have special secretariats attached to them. Commissions of this kind are able to collect and evaluate information, undertake basin-wide studies of water resource development and use, prepare joint strategies and make recommendations to governments. In OECD Europe more than thirty such commissions have been set up to deal with bodies of water and inland regions that bestride frontiers. In North America the USA-Canada International Joint Commission has been in operation since 1911.

A third response of international organisations has been to investigate jointly with their Member countries the economic and trade consequences of environmental policies. Decisions taken by countries to protect their environment can increase the costs of their products and so limit exports or, if they involve product standards, can act as a barrier to imports. International organisations have often helped to prevent trade distortions. In 1972, OECD Member countries reached an agreement on allocating the costs of pollution abatement measures: it was decided that these costs should be borne by polluters, not governments. This "polluter pays principle", which has, by and large, been respected by Member countries, prevented difficulties that would have arisen if some countries had decided to have costs borne by polluters and therefore consumers, while others arranged to have them borne by governments and thus by taxpayers.

International organisations have also helped to prevent environmental constraints from becoming non-tariff barriers to trade. This role is important for a number of products such as cars, food products and chemicals. A growing number of countries, for example, find it necessary to have new chemicals tested prior to their domestic introduction. A common code of good laboratory practice, agreement to undertake tests according to standard methods and other joint actions would lead to more effective environmental protection and to the reduction of potential trade barriers in this important area. The OECD is seeking to lay the foundation for this effort through its Special Programme on the Control of Chemicals.

Enterprise

The demand for a better environment presented enterprises with a challenge that was more direct than that faced by perhaps any other group. Managers in both publicly and privately owned firms responded to new laws, regulations and to changing market conditions by altering production techniques and, to a much lesser extent, by changing the location of their plants. In some countries much remains to be done. The implementation of laws has sometimes been held up by court battles. The effectiveness of them has at other times been weakened by non-compliance. Nevertheless, significant changes have generally taken place. Innovations in production techniques have made it possible to produce a given amount of goods with much less pollution. Earlier pages of this report describe the extent to which some major pollutants have been reduced. These improvements were achieved by the development of new technologies and by the substitution of "clean" for "dirty" ones.

Examples of developments of this kind are numerous: new aircraft emit less noise; new models of cars emit less carbon monoxide, hydrocarbons and nitrogen oxides; new production processes for pulp and paper involve less biological oxygen demand (BOD) in water; and

Table 19.   INVESTMENT (a) BY PRIVATE SECTOR IN CONTROLLING POLLUTION SELECTED COUNTRIES, 1975

	United States	Japan	Denmark	Finland	France	Germany	Netherlands(b)	Norway	Sweden	United Kingdom
% of GDP	0.44	1.00	0.17	0.22	0.28	0.32	0.34	0.22	0.19	0.29
% of total private in-vestment	3.4	4.6	0.9	0.9	1.4	1.9	1.9	0.7	1.1	1.7

(a)   These figures should not be compared without great care because of differences in statistical procedures; for instance, for France and United Kingdom data relating to investments by private sector in controlling pollution have not been collected for this purpose and are estimated from incomplete information.
(b)   1974.

new production processes for caustic soda do not involve the use of mercury at all. The experience of the past decade suggests that the potential for environmental improvement through technological changes is large and often underestimated. Moreover, it is usually resource efficient and often in fact quite profitable.

Some changes have also taken place in the location of industry. The constraints imposed by governments on certain plants, products or emissions are sometimes more severe in certain areas (or in certain countries) than in others, either because assimilative capacities are lower, or because environmental quality objectives are higher. The supply of water or land for various purposes will obviously be more limited in some places than in others, making it more difficult or more costly for firms to settle in them and putting pressure on existing firms to move out. No doubt, some changes in the location of activities, both within countries and between countries, can be attributed to such forces. It is well established however that environmental policies themselves have played a minor role in shaping the location of industry. Production is not in general as mobile as is often assumed, even within a country. Even when it is, environmental considerations are often outweighed in locational decisions by others such as labour costs or transportation.

Changes had been expected to take place in the distribution of investment between developed and developing countries, because of the gap in environmental standards between those two groups of countries. However, in reality it is not easy to find examples of investments that have been located or have shifted to developing countries primarily for environmental reasons. A fortiori, the pattern of investment between OECD countries - where there are smaller differences in environmental constraints - has not been significantly altered by environmental policies.

While environmentally induced redesign of products and processes has led to innovation, cost reduction and increased profit, the abatement of pollution by industry can often entail higher capital investment and operating costs. The ratio of such expenditure by private industry to gross domestic product and to total private investment is available for ten Member countries (Table 19). These costs are difficult to identify for conceptual or practical reasons and available estimates must be treated with caution.

Three points about anti-pollution investment may be made. The first is that such investment is very unevenly distributed amongst industries. In Japan and the United States, for instance, five sectors of production - steel, oil, electricity, pulp and paper, and chemicals - account for about 70 per cent of all anti-pollution

investment.(1) Looked at in another way most of these industries
devoted over 20 per cent of their total investment to anti-pollution
measures. National averages therefore underestimate the significance of anti-pollution investment in several industries.

The second point is that private anti-pollution investment has
increased rapidly during the last decade. In Japan, the ratio of
such investment to gross domestic product more than doubled between
1970 and 1975. In the United States, private anti-pollution investment in constant dollars increased fourfold between 1968 and 1974.
This trend may, however, be levelling off, at least in some countries, such as Japan, where the ratio of anti-pollution investment
to gross domestic product declined in 1977.

A third point may also be made about private anti-pollution
investment. Accelerated depreciation allowances, favourable interest loans, tax deductible funds, and even direct subsidies have
been introduced in many countries to promote such investment. However, the contribution of such schemes to total anti-pollution investment is not high; it was estimated to range between 4.5 per cent
and 14.2 per cent in 1975.(2) This means that, by and large, the
"polluter pays principle" is being applied in Member countries.

Capital expenditure, even though supplemented by current
expenditure, is not a good indicator of the economic cost of pollution abatement for a given year. This can be better defined as
current expenditure plus the depreciation of capital equipment
during the year, together with interest on capital. Estimates on
this basis of the cost of pollution abatement to public and private
industry are available for Japan, the United States, Germany and
Sweden. In Japan, for 1975, such costs represented about 1.7 per
cent of gross domestic product; in the United States, 1.5 per cent
in the same year; in Germany 1.4 per cent in 1974 and in Sweden
0.8 per cent in the same year. These are the most meaningful estimates of the resources allocated to pollution abatement in OECD
countries. They are significantly lower than various other more
fragile estimates that have been made of pollution damage costs.

Figures of the kind just quoted do not tell much about the
economic consequences of pollution abatement. What is a cost to
one firm is income to another, and may well bring additional
business to the first. It is, therefore, hard to pinpoint all the
consequences of pollution abatement policies as they spread through

1) OECD (1977) "Emission Control Costs in the Iron and Steel
   Industry", Paris.
   OECD (1977) "Pollution Control Costs in the Primary Aluminium
   Industry", Paris.

2) Cf. OECD Environment Committee project on the Guiding Principles:
   Procedure for Notification of Financial Assistance Systems for
   Pollution Prevention and Control.

the overall economic system. One way to do it is to simulate the behaviour of an economy, with and without pollution abatement expenditures, using a macro-economic model.(1) Such models have been constructed and utilised in Japan, the United States and the Netherlands. Their conclusions, which are based on current levels of expenditure and current environmental policies, should be accepted with great care, though it will be noted that they all tell a similar story. On the basis of these findings and other information, three additional points can be made.

First, anti-pollution policies do raise prices, but the increases are modest. A Japanese model suggests 0.3 per cent per year. A United States model suggests a similar figure. Of course, higher figures appear for the sectors where pollution abatement costs are higher, and much lower figures for those sectors where costs are low. It may, therefore, be said that on the basis of such estimates pollution abatement policies cannot be held responsible for high rates of inflation.

Second, the adverse effect of price increases on the growth of some sectors is offset by an expansionary impact created by anti-pollution expenditures. In other words, the reduction of activity in polluting industries is offset by development in anti-pollution industries. The net effect on output appears to have been negative in some countries and for certain periods; in other cases it has been positive; however in no instance has it been found important. In the absence of contrary evidence it therefore appears that pollution abatement policies have practically no global impact on economic growth.

Third, the consequences for total employment cannot differ greatly from those for output; and there are some reasons for believing that government spending on pollution control provides more jobs than other forms of investment. In the United States, for instance, it has been calculated that about 60,000 to 70,000 jobs are created for each billion dollars of pollution control spending compared with 50,000 for the average billion of gross national product. The OECD report "Environment Policy in Sweden" indicates that investment in support of environmental policy has been used with some success to foster demand and so combat recession and unemployment.

Evidence about the relationship between environmental policy and the closing of plants and thus unemployment is scant. The few plants closed for environmental reasons have been, by and large, marginal ones that would have been closed anyway and their production was taken over by other, more efficient plants. A detailed

---

1) See OECD (1978) "Employment and Environment", Paris.

analysis of the 1971-78 period in the United States indicates that
fewer than 100 plants were closed because of environmental regulations and that the 20,000 jobs that were lost were more than offset
by the estimated 680,000 jobs created by the implementation of
environmental regulations.

The conclusion seems to be that environmental policy merely
reallocates jobs; it does not reduce them. While such changes inevitably imposed hardship on particular regions, occupations and
industries, in most cases compensating assistance was provided by
governments. On the basis of these observations, it appears that
pollution abatement policies did not contribute to an increase in
total unemployment.

Industry also responded to the environmental challenge by saving
both energy and raw materials. Such savings are clearly beneficial
on two accounts: they conserve scarce resources and they reduce
the problems of waste disposal. There is, of course, a built-in
incentive for private decision makers to save energy and raw materials because they are priced. In addition, many governments have
developed policies recently to encourage more prudent resource
husbandry. During the 1965-75 period, energy consumption increased
more slowly than gross domestic product in countries such as France,
Germany, Japan and the United Kingdom and in most OECD countries
since 1973. Reductions in resource consumption relative to output
are beginning to show up in industrial processes where resource-
efficiency is increasingly scrutinised. As a result, more materials
are being recycled and products recovered and re-used.

CONCLUSIONS

CONCLUSIONS

1.   Over the decade which ended in 1975 most OECD countries experienced rapid economic growth and structural changes: for example, energy use increased by 46 per cent in OECD as a whole, the number of cars in use grew by 75 per cent, the value of agriculture and industry production by respectively 23 and 42 per cent; urban resident levels also grew by about 20 per cent. Heavy pressures were imposed on the environment by this expansion in human activity. Evidence of the damage it was causing heightened public awareness of the environment and led to strenuous demands for a better environment. Governments reacted by passing laws and setting up new institutions to control pollution, manage natural resources and improve towns as places in which to live. In many cases, industry in turn introduced cleaner products and production processes and stepped up its efforts to conserve resources. In reality the action and interaction of citizens, government and industry were more complex than this but there is no doubt the challenge to the environment was faced.

2.   How effectively has it been faced?
    This first report has assessed changes in the state of the environment in Member countries over the past decade. It is based on a number of national reviews, previous work by the Organisation and additional information. On the strength of that assessment, it is possible to describe broad trends, successes achieved and remaining problems; to show how attitudes are changing; and to demonstrate the need to deepen and extend scientific knowledge, improve statistics and develop reporting on the state of the environment in Member countries. The conclusions drawn do not, of course, necessarily apply to every Member country.

ENVIRONMENTAL TRENDS, SUCCESSES AND REMAINING PROBLEMS

3.   Significant progress was made in dealing with environmental problems identified as most important and made the object of sustained effort during the late sixties and early seventies. The report identifies the following improvements in environmental quality:

- reduced water pollution by suspended solids and biodegradable oxidisable matter;
- reduced urban air pollution by sulphur dioxides, particulate matter, and containment of urban air pollution by carbon monoxide;
- reduced flows in the environment of some persistent chemicals such as DDT, PCB's and alkylmercury compounds, and reduction or stabilization of them in most samples of wildlife;
- extended protection of outstanding rural environments by their designation and management as national or regional parks;
- extended protection of the built environment through the creation of pedestrian streets and traffic management in central and residential areas; extended protection and rehabilitation of buildings of outstanding historical or architectural value.

These improvements were not always easily obtained. Their extent varies from country to country and some actions were unsuccessful. Furthermore the extent of success is not fully reflected in the environmental improvements themselves. Its full scale becomes clear only if the improvements are considered in the light of the deterioration that would have occurred had nothing been done.

4. Studies in several countries indicate that the cost in economic terms of the environmental improvements already achieved has been moderate. National resources allocated to pollution abatement were nowhere estimated to be higher than 1.7 per cent of gross domestic product in the mid-1970s. Only moderate consequences for total employment, prices and economic growth can be identified, though more severe effects were felt in some industries and some regions. However, the need for large-scale investment by some industries resulted in the spin-off of cleaner and in some cases more efficient technologies.

5. Certain forms of environmental damage, that received less attention and for which policies were more difficult to define, have got worse, or at best, have often only been checked. Evidence shows that environmental quality has tended to deteriorate in various places in the following ways:

- the quality of drinking water is the subject of increasing concern and the eutrophication of lakes has in many countries become more widespread;
- air pollution by photochemical oxidants has become of concern and emissions of nitrogen oxides have increased;
- noise has become more pervasive and insistent, and large numbers of people are now exposed to levels interfering with their daily life;

- some land has deteriorated due to erosion, increased aridity, and abandonment and good quality farm land has been lost to urban uses.

6.   The changes in the state of the environment may be further characterised as follows:

- action on a limited set of pollutants has led to identification of a wider range of substances potentially damaging to the environment;
- the emission of pollutants from point sources such as chimneys and sewage outfalls has often declined, but emissions from diffused sources have generally increased;
- the degree of concentration of some pollutants at "black spots" has often been reduced or stabilized, but some pollutants, such as those sulphur compounds that are transported long distances by air, now affect much wider areas;
- some tracts of land are now well protected, but concern for better nationwide land management has grown;
- acute ill-health and death caused by short-term exposure to intense loads of pollution have generally decreased but risks to humans of long-term effects from exposure to substances that may give rise to genetic changes, cancer and deformities at birth are receiving increased attention;
- during the past 10 years there have been many accidents involving toxic chemicals and oil; the amount of oil accidentally released in marine waters has increased recently; these accidents have caused damage to the environment and economic losses.

CHANGING ATTITUDES

7.   Concern about the quality of life has grown amongst the public and has been increasingly recognised by governments in recent years. Public attitudes towards the environment relative to other concerns are indicated by opinion surveys in North America and a number of European countries. These show that, in the present economic context, support for measures to improve the environment remains high, third only to reducing inflation and unemployment. Recent surveys in North America indicate that a majority of people would be prepared to pay more in retail prices and taxes to sustain a high quality environment rather than have higher incomes and live in a poorer environment. Similar findings have been observed in Japan.

8.   There is some evidence that the relationship between resource consumption and output is improving. This appears to be due both to the effects of the market and to changing attitudes about the

management of resources and wastes by government, industry and the public. Reductions in resource consumption relative to gross domestic product are particularly apparent in the case of energy; they are also beginning to show in industrial processes where resource-efficiency standards have been defined, materials are being recycled and products are being recovered and re-used.

9. Other economic and social changes are taking place that have major implications for the environment. Amongst them are further increases in incomes, mobility, and leisure and trends to suburban expansion, second homes, and more spread-out forms of industrial production; all these are likely to add to demands for land and energy. Such changes coupled with higher levels of education can in turn be expected to increase public support for environmental measures.

10. Thus it will not be enough to go on applying effort where it has been successful and to intensifying it where it has not. Future efforts will have to be set in the context of social and economic change and aimed at the prudent husbandry of all natural resources and the improvement of the quality of life.

THE NEED FOR BETTER ENVIRONMENTAL INFORMATION

11. Improvements to the collection, interpretation and publication of environmental facts are essential to the further control of pollution, the successful management of natural resources and the improvement of man's quality of life. Accurate, appropriate and internationally comparable facts enable the outcome of past actions to be assessed, new initiatives to be taken and national policies to be harmonized. They permit the environmental consequences of actions to be taken into account in decision making and, when publicised, they satisfy the public "right to know". Further improvements to man's habitat are therefore dependent on the production of better environmental information.

12. Today, national year books of environmental statistics,[1] national reports on the state of the environment[2] and the work of

---

1) OECD 1978, "State of Environmental Statistics", Paris. Such year books have been published in Austria, Canada, Finland, France, Japan, Netherlands, Norway, Sweden, United Kingdom, United States and Yugoslavia.

2) Reports have been published in France, Germany, Italy, Japan, Luxembourg, Netherlands, Spain, Sweden, United States and Yugoslavia.

international organisations provide a foundation for the production of such information. At an international level, they provide a format for the development of a core of environmental statistics and indicators and for the exchange of experience on techniques such as the monitoring of pollutants, remote sensing, ecological mapping, attitude studies and special surveys and inventories.

13. The inadequacy of data on recently recognised environmental issues needs to be made good. Improved data are required on trends in background levels of pollutants, trends in micro-pollutants in fresh and coastal waters, and on the effects of air pollution on the ecosystem, the climate and the stratosphere. The emission, concentration and long-term effect of persistent chemicals; trends in the exposure of people to noise and its related effects, and facts on the state of the wildlife and on the evolution of ecosystems are other fields where better data are needed. Finally there are gaps that remain to be filled in information on evironmental expenditure, on environmental damages and benefits, on the provision of amenities, and on changes in natural resources in time and space.

14. There are some cases where environmental data exist but are not sufficiently related to policy-making, action and environmental assessments. On certain problems there is a need to improve scientific knowledge. Without this better understanding, it is difficult to determine what information to collect, what phenomena to monitor and how to interpret any results.

15. Given these circumstances there is a need for determined action to overcome institutional, administrative and financial barriers to the development of environmental information, and to find internationally acceptable ways of analysing and accounting for stocks of natural resources, amenities and wastes. Current work in OECD, including the preparation of the Draft Recommendation on "Reporting on the State of the Environment", is aimed at meeting this need.

TECHNICAL ANNEXES

Annex 1. GROWTH IN THE VALUE OF AGRICULTURAL PRODUCTION[a], OECD COUNTRIES, 1965–1975

COUNTRY	FOOD COMMODITIES			ALL AGRICULTURAL COMMODITIES		
	PRODUCTION INDEX[b]		% CHANGE	PRODUCTION INDEX[c]		% CHANGE
	1965	1975	1965-1975	1965	1975	1965-1975
Canada	113	122	8	112	122	9
USA	105	137	30	103	129	25
Japan	104	131	26	103	129	25
Australia	102	144	41	103	131	27
New Zealand	105	127	21	107	119	11
Austria	92	119	29	92	119	29
Belgium	96	118	23	96	116	21
Denmark	102	106	4	102	106	4
Finland	106	114	8	106	114	8
France	108	124	15	108	124	15
Germany	98	121	23	98	121	23
Greece	114	161	41	113	154	36
Iceland	103	115	12	103	110	7
Ireland	96	133	39	96	132	38
Italy	106	124	17	106	124	17
Luxembourg	97	113	16	97	113	16
Netherlands	98	151	54	98	149	52
Norway	100	109	9	100	108	8
Portugal	107	108	1	107	108	1
Spain	99	158	60	98	154	57
Sweden	101	109	8	101	109	8
Switzerland	96	117	22	96	117	22
Turkey	100	142	42	101	155	53
United Kingdom	106	121	14	106	121	14
North America	105	135	29	104	128	23
Australia and New Zealand	103	139	35	104	128	23
OECD Europe	103	127	23	103	128	24
OECD Total	104	132	27	104	128	23

NOTES: a) The data refer to FAO production index series constructed by applying regional weights based on 1961-1965 price relationships to the country production figures. Deductions were made for feed and seed used in the production process. 1961-1965 = 100.

b) The food index relates to the production of crops and livestock products for human consumption.

c) The "all commodities" index includes in addition fibres, tobacco, industrial oilseeds and rubber.

SOURCE: FAO (1976), "Production Yearbook 1975", Volume 29, Rome.

Annex 2. COMPOSITION OF AGRICULTURAL PRODUCTION[a], AS A PERCENTAGE OF THE TOTAL, SELECTED COUNTRIES, AVERAGE FOR 1973 AND 1974

COUNTRY	VEGETAL PRODUCTION			ANIMAL PRODUCTION			
	CEREALS (1)	OTHER VEGETAL PRODUCTS (2)	TOTAL VEGETAL PRODUCTION (3) = (1)+(2)	MILK AND DAIRY PRODUCTS (4)	MEAT AND LIVE ANIMALS (5)	OTHER ANIMAL PRODUCTS (6)	TOTAL ANIMAL PRODUCTION (7) = (4)+(5)+(6)
Canada	31.9[b]	15.8	47.7	15.8	27.4	9.1	52.3
USA	23.9	29.8	53.7	10.6	32.0	3.7	46.3
Japan	38.4	33.6	72.0	5.3	19.6	3.1	28.0
Australia	..	..	49.2	9.0	20.8	21.0	50.8
New Zealand ...	5.7[c]	5.4[d]	11.1	21.7	46.8	20.4	88.9
Austria	7.2	23.6	30.8	20.1	44.6	4.5	69.2
Belgium	5.3	28.3	33.6	16.3	45.4	4.7	66.4
Denmark	14.6	10.9	25.5	24.9	48.1	1.5	74.5
Finland	14.3	3.1	17.5	42.5	33.7	6.3	82.5
France	17.0	28.6	45.6	16.5	35.1	2.9	54.4
Germany	8.5	21.7	30.2	22.9	41.0	5.9	69.8
Ireland	6.7	8.6	15.3	27.6	54.4	2.7	84.7
Italy	12.5	48.9	61.4	10.0	24.8	3.8	38.6
Luxembourg ...	5.7	14.8	20.5	37.5	38.6	3.4	79.5
Netherlands ...	2.5	30.7	33.2	26.8	36.6	3.4	66.8
Norway	11.6	15.9	27.5	37.7	29.0	5.8	72.5
Portugal	45.2	39.2	84.4	3.0	8.4	4.2	15.6
Spain	10.6	48.2	58.8	9.3	27.0	4.9	41.2
Switzerland ...	5.2	16.4	21.6	31.6	46.2	0.6	78.4
United Kingdom .	14.2	19.2	33.4	21.1	37.9	7.6	66.6

NOTES: a) Figures exclude the value of products used as raw materials for agricultural production (e.g. as feed and seed) on the farm where they were produced or after being traded between farms. Products sold to dealers or processors and later bought by farms for inputs are included in the figures. Columns (3) and (7) add up to 100%.
b) Wheat, oats and barley only.
c) Grains and field crops.
d) Fruit and vegetables.

COUNTRY	AGRICULTU-RAL LAND[a] 1975 (THOUSAND KM^2)	AGRICULTURAL WORKERS			
		THOUSANDS OF WORKERS		PER KM^2 OF AGRICULTURAL LAND	
		1965	1975	1965	1975
Canada	636	786	617	1.2	1.0
USA	4,350	4,050	2,598	0.9	0.6
Japan	58	12,921	10,492	222.2	180.5
Australia	5,007	450	394	0.1	0.1
New Zealand	139	132	128	1.0	0.9
Austria	38	626	380	16.5	10.0
Belgium	15	230	144	15.1	9.4
Denmark	29	319	212	10.9	7.2
Finland	28	603	376	21.5	13.4
France	323	3,664	2,433	11.3	7.5
Germany	128	2,902	1,536	22.7	12.0
Greece	89	1,946	1,582	22.0	17.9
Iceland[b]	23	16	13	0.7	0.6
Ireland	48	349	280	7.2	5.8
Italy	175	5,023	3,031	28.7	17.3
Luxembourg	13	15	8	1.2	0.6
Netherlands	21	426	342	20.4	16.4
Norway	9	225	146	25.1	16.3
Portugal	42	1,388	1,012	33.1	24.1
Spain	281	3,980	2,620	14.2	9.3
Sweden	37	379	235	10.2	6.3
Switzerland	20	256	198	12.7	9.8
Turkey	538	10,692	10,455	19.9	19.4
United Kingdom	186	864	615	4.7	3.3
North America	4,986	4,836	3,215	1.0	0.6
Australia and New Zealand	5,146	582	522	0.1	0.1
OECD Europe	2,043	33,903	25,618	16.6	12.5
OECD Total	12,234	52,242	39,847	4.3	3.3

NOTES: a) Agricultural land refers to total arable, crop and permanent grassland as given in Annex 20.
  b) Permanent grassland only.
SOURCE: FAO (1976), "Production Yearbook 1975", Volume 29, Rome.

Annex 4. TRACTORS AND COMBINED HARVESTER-THRESHERS IN USE[a], TOTAL AND PER KM2 OF ARABLE AND CROPLAND, OECD COUNTRIES, 1965-1975

COUNTRY	ARABLE AND CROPLAND[c] 1975 (THOUSAND KM2)	TRACTORS AND COMBINED HARVESTER-THRESHERS IN USE			
		THOUSANDS OF MACHINES		MACHINES PER KM2 OF AGRICULTURAL LAND[c]	
		1965[b]	1975	1965[b]	1975
Canada	393	728	812	1.9	2.1
USA	1,910	5,690	4,764	3.0	2.5
Japan	56	27	694	0.5	12.5
Australia	450	348	397	0.8	0.9
New Zealand	10	93	103	9.4	10.5
Austria	16	181	321	11.3	19.9
Belgium and Luxembourg	9	70	113	8.1	13.0
Denmark	27	167	230	6.3	8.7
Finland	26	120	227	4.5	8.6
France	189	953	1,498	5.0	7.9
Germany	75	1,150	1,613	15.3	21.4
Greece	39	32	92	0.8	2.3
Iceland	..	7	10	..	..
Ireland	12	57	115	4.6	9.2
Italy	123	352	847	2.9	6.9
Netherlands	9	111	188	13.0	22.2
Norway	8	71	119	9.0	15.1
Portugal	37	14	54	0.4	1.5
Spain	208	121	419	0.6	2.0
Sweden	30	193	237	6.4	7.9
Switzerland	4	62	88	16.2	22.9
Turkey	277	54	232	0.2	0.8
United Kingdom	70	534	555	7.7	8.0
North America	2,303	6,418	5,576	2.8	2.4
Australia and New Zealand	460	441	500	1.0	1.1
OECD Europe	1,159	4,243	6,856	3.7	5.9
OECD Total	3,977	11,136	13,637	2.8	3.4

NOTES: a) The data refer to both wheel and crawler tractors used in agriculture and to combined harvesters-threshers. Wheel tractors are generally limited to those having three or four wheels and engines of over 8 HP. Crawler or track-layer type tractors are also generally limited to those over 8 HP. Combined harvester-threshers are generally limited to those machines which reap and thresh in one operation.

b) The figures for 1965 refer to the average number of machines in use over the period 1961-1965.

c) The assumption that all tractors are used exclusively on arable and cropland (as given in Annex 20) is less satisfactory for countries where such machines play an important role in livestock rearing and forestry.

SOURCE: UNO (1976), "Statistical Yearbook 1975", New York.

COUNTRY	ARABLE AND CROPLAND [d] 1975 (THOUSAND KM^2)	COMMERCIAL FERTILIZER (NPK) CONSUMED [d]			
		THOUSAND METRIC TONS		METRIC TONS PER KM^2 OF ARABLE AND CROPLAND [d]	
		1965 [c]	1975	1965 [c]	1975
Canada	393	523	1,303	1.3	3.3
USA	1,910	9,391	18,840	4.9	9.9
Japan	56	1,799	1,779	32.3	31.9
Australia	450	826	728	1.8	1.6
New Zealand	10	369	490	37.3	49.6
Austria	16	304	310	18.9	19.3
Belgium and Luxembourg	9	446	464	51.3	53.4
Denmark	27	455	639	17.1	24.0
Finland	26	283	516	10.7	19.6
France	189	2,821	4,640	14.9	24.5
Germany	75	2,627	3,107	34.9	41.2
Greece	39	215	463	5.5	11.8
Iceland	..	17	28	..	..
Ireland	12	224	429	18.0	34.4
Italy	123	931	1,490	7.6	12.1
Netherlands	9	531	626	62.4	73.6
Norway	8	158	230	19.9	29.0
Portugal	37	158	245	4.3	6.7
Spain	208	756	1,443	3.6	6.9
Sweden	30	340	523	11.3	17.4
Switzerland	4	121	138	31.5	36.0
Turkey	277	101	842	0.4	3.0
United Kingdom	70	1,464	1,835	21.0	26.4
North America	2,303	9,914	20,143	4.3	8.8
Australia and New Zealand	460	1,195	1,218	2.6	2.7
OECD Europe	1,159	11,949	17,967	10.3	15.5
OECD Total	3,977	24,856	41,108	6.3	10,3

NOTES: a) The data refer to the nitrogen (N) content of commercial inorganic fertilizers; commercial phosphoric acid (P_2O_5) which covers the P_2O_5 content of superphosphates, ammonium phosphate and basic slag but excludes the P_2O_5 content of ground natural phosphate to avoid duplication; and the K_2O content of commercial potash; muriate, nitrate and sulphate of potash, manure salts, kainit and nitrate of soda potash.

b) Years relate to twelve-month periods 1 July-30 June.

c) The data for 1965 refer to the average consumption of commercial (NPK) fertilizers over the period 1961-1965.

d) The assumption that all of the fertilizer consumed is applied exclusively to arable and cropland (as given in Annex 20) is less satisfactory for countries where significant amounts of such fertilizers are applied to permanent grasslands or forestland.

SOURCE: UNO (1976), "Statistical Yearbook 1975", New York.

Annex 6. CONSUMPTION OF COMMERCIAL NITROGENOUS FERTILIZERS[a], TOTAL AND PER KM^2 OF ARABLE AND CROPLAND, OECD COUNTRIES, 1965-1975 [b]

COUNTRY	ARABLE AND CROPLAND[d] 1975 (THOUSAND KM^2	CONSUMPTION OF COMMERCIAL NITROGENOUS FERTILIZERS[d]			
		THOUSAND METRIC TONS		METRIC TONS PER KM^2 OF ARABLE AND CROPLAND[d]	
		1965[c]	1975	1965[c]	1975
Canada	393	152	562	0.4	1.4
USA	1,910	3,922	9,385	2.1	4.9
Japan	56	736	638	13.2	11.5
Australia	450	57	165	0.1	0.4
New Zealand	10	5	10	0.5	1.0
Austria	16	70	121	4.4	7.6
Belgium and Luxembourg	9	140	182	16.1	20.9
Denmark	27	158	339	5.9	12.8
Finland	26	79	199	3.0	7.6
France	189	766	1,708	4.1	9.0
Germany	75	760	1,228	10.1	16.3
Greece	39	112	275	2.9	7.0
Iceland	..	9	15	..	..
Ireland	12	32	153	2.5	12.2
Italy	123	393	724	3.2	5.9
Netherlands	9	286	453	33.7	53.3
Norway	8	58	98	7.3	12.4
Portugal	37	82	375	2.2	10.2
Spain	208	351	763	1.7	3.7
Sweden	30	134	257	4.5	8.5
Switzerland	4	22	42	5.7	11.0
Turkey	277	54	453	0.2	1.6
United Kingdom	70	581	1,045	8.4	15.0
North America	2,303	4,074	9,947	1.8	4.3
Australia and New Zealand	460	61	175	0.1	0.4
OECD Europe	1,159	4,086	8,430	3.5	7.3
OECD Total	3,977	8,957	19,190	2.3	4.8

NOTES: a) The data refer to the nitrogen (N) content of commercial inorganic fertilizers only.

b) Years relate to twelve-month periods 1 July-30 June.

c) The data for 1965 refer to the average consumption of commercial nitrogenous (N) fertilizers over the period 1961-1965.

d) The assumption that all of the fertilizer consumed is applied exclusively to arable and cropland (as given in Annex 20) is less satisfactory for countries where significant amounts of such fertilizers are applied to permanent grassland or forestland.

SOURCE: UNO (1976), "Statistical Yearbook 1975", New York.

Annex 7. CATCHES OF MARINE FISH, CRUSTACEANS AND CEPHALOPODS, [a] BY MAJOR MARINE AREAS, 1965, 1970 AND 1975

MARINE AREAS	CATCHES (THOUSAND METRIC TONS)		
	1965	1970	1975
N.W. Atlantic [b]	3,242	3,697	3,230
N.E. Atlantic	9,090	10,140	11,499
W.C. Atlantic	1,192	1,202	1,350
E.C. Atlantic	1,216	2,981	3,493
Mediterranean and Black Sea	940	1,040	1,236
S.W. Atlantic	489	1,032	824
S.E. Atlantic	2,213	2,453	2,535
W. Indian Ocean	1,238	1,583	2,029
E. Indian Ocean	628	779	1,042
N.W. Pacific	9,540	11,834	15,201
N.E. Pacific	1,420	2,609	2,206
W.C. Pacific	2,560	3,923	4,637
E.C. Pacific	575	861	1,233
S.W. Pacific	101	144	258
S.E. Pacific [b]	8,054	13,621	4,516
Total	42,498	57,705	55,289

NOTES: a) Molluscs other than cephalopods (oysters, mussels, clams, etc.) are excluded because their potential depends more on cultivation than on natural factors.
   b) Former overexploitation.

SOURCE: FAO (1976), "Review of the State of Exploitation of the World Fish Resources", Rome.

Annex 8. FISH PRODUCTION BY USE, OECD COUNTRIES, 1976

COUNTRY	FISH PRODUCTION (THOUSAND TONS)			FISH MEAL PRODUCTION (THOUSAND TONS)
	FOOD	INDUSTRIAL	TOTAL	
Canada	1,015	87	1,102	51
USA	1,252	1,175	2,427	262
Japan	9,626	1,070	10,695	500
Australia [a]	102	12[b]	114[b]	..
New Zealand	54	10	63	..
Belgium	45	–	45	3
Denmark	387	1,536	1,923[c]	325
Finland	52	38[b]	90[b]	..
France	690	2	691	19
Germany	397	34	431	61
Greece	122	–	122	–
Iceland	510	473	982	109
Ireland	63	18	81	..
Italy	374	2	377	..
Netherlands	237	9	246	..
Norway	54	10	63	464
Portugal	267	20	287	..
Spain	1,366	152	1,518	30
Sweden	132	70	202	10
Turkey[d]	244	16	260	..
United Kingdom	779	153	933	115
North America	2,267	1,262	3,529	313
Australia and New Zealand	156	22	177	..
OECD Europe	5,719	2,533	8,251	1,136
OECD Total	17,768	4,887	22,652	1,950
OECD Total as a % of World Total	..	..	32 %	51 %

NOTES: a) 1975-1976.

b) Estimated.

c) Including an estimated 44,600 tons of fish for food concerning Greenland.

d) 1975.

Annex 9.   INDUSTRIAL PRODUCTION INDICES[a],
TOTAL OUTPUT AND SELECTED INDUSTRIES, OECD COUNTRIES, 1965 AND 1975

COUNTRY	TOTAL INDUSTRIAL PRODUCTION[b]		CHEMICALS, RUBBER AND PETROLEUM AND COAL PRODUCTS		IRON AND STEEL		TEXTILES, CLOTHING AND LEATHER		FOOD, BEVERAGES AND TOBACCO	
	1965	1975	1965	1975	1965	1975	1965	1975	1965	1975
Canada	79	120	77	125	84	111	88	113	83	115
USA	84	107	71	119	101	91	98	98	84	112
Japan	49	110	45	113	43	111	73	93	74	111
Australia	79	110	67	125	78[c]	113[c]	87	100	78	119
New Zealand	..	..	..	..	..	..	..	..	..	..
Austria	73	118	66	129	78	98	80	103	78	113
Belgium	81	108	67	117	78	86	89	93	80	120
Denmark	..	..	..	..	..	..	..	..	..	..
Finland	69	122	62	129	66[c]	134[c]	68	120	71	115
France	76	112	67	111	83	92	90	101	87	112
Germany	78	105	64	110	80	90	95	94	83	114
Greece	62	151	44	164	34[c]	159[c]	73	172	83	119
Iceland	..	..	..	..	..	..	..	..	..	..
Ireland	71	115	57	144	79[d]	110[d]	68	105	78	120
Italy	70	109	65	115	70	119	81	102	79	115
Luxembourg	87	93	57	112	86[c]	81[c]	..	..	83	119
Netherlands	66	115	51	117	60[c]	100[c]	101	73	80	118
Norway	80	128	77	116	71[c]	115[c]	103	84	92	106
Portugal	..	..	..	..	..	..	..	..	..	..
Spain	60	140	54	157	47	167	76	100	58	124
Sweden	79	115	61	118	79	102	100	85	82	104
Switzerland	76	97	63	111	72[d]	96[d]	95	89	80	101
Turkey	..	..	..	..	..	..	..	..	..	..
United Kingdom	89	103	72	108	103	75	100	99	87	108
North America	83	108	71	119	99	93	97	99	84	113
OECD Europe	77	109	65	114	81	95	90	99	81	114
OECD Total	77	109	65	116	82	97	91	98	81	113

NOTES: a) 1970 = 100.
  b) The total index comprises in principle mining and quarrying, manufacturing and gas, electricity and water but no standard measure of the index is available for all countries.
  c) Data relates to all basic metals.
  d) Data relates to all metal products.

Annex 10. PRODUCTION AND ASSEMBLY OF MOTOR VEHICLES[a], OECD COUNTRIES, 1965, 1970 AND 1975

COUNTRY	NUMBER OF VEHICLES 1975 (IN THOUSANDS)	CHANGE IN OUTPUT 1965 = 100	
		1970	1975
Canada	1,443	137	170
USA	8,987	75	81
Japan	6,942	276	362
Australia	456	137	131
New Zealand	116 [b]	108	161
Austria	8	88	160
Belgium	848 [b]	154	165
Denmark	8	50	24
Finland	..	..	..
France	3,300	170	204
Germany	3,186	129	107
Greece	..	73	..
Iceland	–	–	–
Ireland	62	109	132
Italy	1,459	158	124
Luxembourg	–	–	–
Netherlands	74	219	206
Norway	–	–	–
Portugal	..	163	..
Spain	814	229	351
Sweden	367	149	180
Switzerland	..	116	..
Turkey	73	480	2,086
United Kingdom	1,648	96	76
North America	10,430	79	88
Australia and New Zealand	572	133	138
OECD Europe	11,847	137	131
OECD Total	29,791	119	128

NOTES: a) Cars, buses and coaches, and goods vehicles.

b) 1974.

SOURCE: International Road Federation (1977), "World Road Statistics 1972-75", Washington D.C.

COUNTRY	THOUSANDS OF INHABITANTS[a]			MILLIONS OF URBAN RESIDENTS[b]			LEVEL OF URBANISATION (%)	
	1965	1975	% CHANGE 1965-1975	1965	1975	% CHANGE 1965-1975	1965	1975
Canada	19,678	22,831	16.0	13.0[c]	15.6[c]	21	66	69
USA	194,303	213,540	9.9	125.0	151.3	21	64	71
Japan	97,950	111,566	13.9	74.4[c]	88.8[c]	19	76	80
Australia	11,341	13,771	21.4	8.0[c]	9.7[c]	22	70	70
New Zealand	2,635	3,087	17.2	1.7	2.1	24	66	69
Austria	7,291	7,520	3.1	2.8	2.9	5	38	39
Belgium	9,508	9,801	3.1	4.5	4.7	5	47	48
Denmark	4,797	5,060	5.5	2.5[c]	2.5[c]	-	52	49
Finland	4,581	4,712	2.9	1.6	2.3[c]	42	35	49
France	49,164	52,748	7.3	25.5	30.0	17	52	57
Germany	59,148	61,825	4.5	29.1	36.8	27	49	60
Greece	8,614	9,046	5.0	3.7	4.8	29	43	53
Iceland	196	218	11.2	0.1	0.1	10	46	45
Ireland	2,884	3,127	8.4	1.0	1.2	17	35	37
Italy	52,332	55,812	6.7	26.5	32.6	23	51	58
Luxembourg	334	358	7.2	0.1	0.1	-	31	29
Netherlands	12,455	13,654	9.6	7.6	8.8	17	61	65
Norway	3,753	4,007	6.8	1.5[c]	1.7[c]	17	39	42
Portugal	9,109	9,426	3.5	1.9[c]	2.6[c]	37	21	28
Spain	32,394	35,814	10.6	16.4	21.2	30	51	59
Sweden	7,807	8,196	5.0	4.1[c]	4.6[c]	13	53	56
Switzerland	5,996	6,405	6.8	1.8	1.9	6	31	30
Turkey	31,934	40,025	25.3	8.1	12.3	51	25	31
United Kingdom	54,653	56,043	2.5	38.5	39.8	3	70	71
North America	213,981	236,371	10.5	137.9	166.9	21	65	71
Australia and New Zealand ..	13,976	16,858	20.6	9.7	11.8	22	69	70
OECD Europe	353,746	383,801	8.5	177.2	210.8	19	50	55
OECD Total	679,653	748,596	10.1	399.1	478.4	20	59	64

NOTES: a) OECD mid-year estimates of national populations.

   b) OECD estimates of urban populations in settlements of 20,000 or more inhabitants (based on national contributions and national publications) unless otherwise specified.

   c) Data supplied by Member countries.

CONVENTIONAL DWELLINGS OCCUPIED (MILLIONS)		COUNTRY	MOTORWAY NETWORKS[c] (KILOMETRES)		MAIN OR NATIONAL ROADS[c] (KILOMETRES)	
1965	1975		1965	1975	1965	1975
5.18	7.49	Canada	2,043	..	..	276,800
55.70[a]	71.64[a]	USA	31,192	64,653	666,250	772,812
20.37[b]	28.73[b]	Japan	342	1,615	27,858	38,539
3.15	4.28[a]	Australia	..	..	97,959	120,593
0.72	0.93	New Zealand	64	108	11,418	10,691
2.46	2.88	Austria	334	651	9,234	9,119
3.37	3.88	Belgium	310	1,018	10,148	10,832
1.63	2.02	Denmark	102	345	..	4,313
1.34	1.62	Finland	36	174	8,987	9,986
17.10	21.08	France	642	3,401	..	27,489
19.02	23.62	Germany	3,372	6,200	30,000	32,500
2.25[a]	3.08[a]	Greece	..	91	7,693	8,631
0.05[a]	0.06	Iceland	..	..	3,041	3,689
0.69	0.81	Ireland	..	..	..	2,603
15.74	18.39	Italy	1,706	5,431	37,844	44,234
0.10	0.13	Luxembourg	..	25	865	865
3.26	4.42	Netherlands	568	1,530	45,572	51,338
1.17[a]	1.41[a]	Norway	22	165	23,191	24,897
2.25a	2.36[a]	Portugal	66	66	5,574	18,548
8.63	12.16	Spain	60	1,135	..	78,286
2.88	3.53	Sweden	223	692	11,820	12,470
1.85	2.52	Switzerland	106	662	17,600	18,158
3.27[a]	3.92	Turkey	..	189	29,557	33,762
17.78	20.35	United Kingdom	566[d]	2,024[d]	13,434[d]	13,480[d]
60.88	79.13	North America	..	..		
3.87	5.21	Australia and New Zealand	..	..		
104.84	128.24	OECD Europe	8,124[e]	23,585[e]		
189.96	241.31	OECD Total	39,722[e]	89,961[e]		

NOTES: a) OECD estimates made on the basis of information in national and international publications.

b) 1963-1973.

c) Data are not strictly comparable because of differences in definitions between countries or the reclassification of roads during the period 1965-1975.

d) Great Britain only.

e) Partial totals.

SOURCES: UNO (1977), "Yearbook of construction statistics 1966-1975", New York.

UNO-ECE (1978), "Annual Bulletin of Housing and Building Statistics for Europe 1977", New York.

UNO (1976), "Compendium of Housing Statistics 1972-74", New York.

International Road Federation (1977), "World Road Statistics 1972-76", Washington, D.C.

GROWTH IN STOCKS OF PASSENGER CARS IN USE, TOTAL AND PER 1,000 INHABITANTS, OECD COUNTRIES, 1965-1975

COUNTRY	PASSANGER CARS IN USE[a]			CARS PER 1,000 INHABITANTS	
	1965	1975	% CHANGE 1965-1975	1965	1975
Canada	5.28	8.87	70	268	389
USA	74.90	106.08	43	385	497
Japan	2.20	17.24	684	22	154
Australia	2.90	5.01	73	255	364
New Zealand	0.72	1.17	63	272	378
Austria	0.79	1.72	118	108	229
Belgium	1.34	2.61	95	141	267
Denmark	0.74	1.30	74	155	257
Finland	0.45	1.00	119	99	211
France	9.60	15.30	62	195	290
Germany	8.98	17.90	99	152	289
Greece	0.10	0.44	321	12	49
Iceland	0.03	0.06	126	144	293
Ireland	0.28	0.52	81	99	165
Italy	5.47	15.06	175	105	270
Luxembourg	0.06	0.11	127	185	321
Netherlands	1.27	3.40	167	102	249
Norway	0.47	0.95	105	124	238
Portugal	0.32	0.94	194	35	99
Spain	0.81	4.81	495	25	134
Sweden	1.79	2.76	54	230	337
Switzerland	0.92	1.79	95	153	280
Turkey	0.09	0.38	350	3	10
United Kingdom	9.25	14.26	54	169	255
North America	80.18	116.33	45	375	492
Australia and New Zealand	3.61	6.18	71	258	367
OECD Europe	42.77	85.57	100	121	223
OECD Total	128.76	225.32	75	189	301

NOTE: a) Millions of passenger cars in use at the end of the year.

SOURCE: International Road Federation (1977), "World Road Statistics 1972-76", Washington D.C.

Annex 14. GROWTH IN ROAD PASSENGER AND GOODS TRANSPORT, SELECTED COUNTRIES, 1965-1975

MILLIONS OF PASSENGER KILOMETRES TRAVELLED BY PRIVATE ROAD TRANSPORT		COUNTRY	MILLIONS OF TON KILOMETRES TRANSPORTED BY ROAD	
1965	1975		1965	1975
64,000	..	Canada	..	36,280
1,315,764	3,308,000	USA	526,686	646,628
40,600	250,900	Japan	48,400	129,700
..	153,800	Australia	15,800	33,000
12,426	23,376[a]	New Zealand	4,512[b]	6,168[a]
24,083	30,652	Belgium	8,532	16,521
33,000	39,400[a]	Denmark	9,700	9,000[a]
11,400	28,300[a]	Finland	8,000	15,700[a]
184,000	364,000	France	46,900	90,000
265,600	462,700	Germany	62,500	92,900
81,219	279,259	Italy	45,788	62,795
52,680	102,900	Netherlands	8,901	15,300
6,865	25,794	Norway	2,645	4,371[c]
36,164[b]	99,330	Spain	18,612[b]	76,500
45,000	67,000	Sweden	13,000	22,100
23,520	68,230	Turkey	7,939	23,360
232,800	357,000	United Kingdom	68,800	88,300

NOTES: a) 1973.
      b) 1967.
      c) 1974.

SOURCES: International Road Federation (1977), "World Road Statistics 1972-1976", Washington D.C.
Bureau Permanent International des Constructeurs d'Automobiles (1977), "Le Rôle de l'Automobile dans l'Economie Industrielle Moderne", Paris.

Annex 15. GROWTH IN ENERGY CONSUMPTION[a], TOTAL AND PER CAPITA, OECD COUNTRIES, 1965-1975

COUNTRY	1965	1975	% INCREASE 1965-1975	PER CAPITA ENERGY CONSUMPTION[b]	
				1965	1975
Canada	118.4	200.5	69	6.0	8.8
USA	1,225.5	1,690.1	38	6.3	7.9
Japan	151.4	331.9	119	1.5	3.0
Australia	37.1	59.4	60	3.3	4.3
New Zealand	7.0	10.1	44	2.7	3.3
Austria	15.7	22.9	46	2.2	3.0
Belgium	31.7	41.8	32	3.3	4.3
Denmark	13.7	17.7	29	2.9	3.5
Finland	14.6	22.3	53	3.2	4.7
France	116.2	168.1	45	2.4	3.2
Germany	184.6	243.5	32	3.1	3.9
Greece	5.0	11.8	136	0.6	1.3
Iceland	0.7	1.1	57	3.6	5.0
Ireland	4.6	7.1	54	1.6	2.3
Italy	74.0	127.0	72	1.4	2.3
Luxembourg	3.9	4.0	3	11.7	11.2
Netherlands	31.8	59.0	86	2.6	4.3
Norway	12.9	19.1	48	3.4	4.8
Portugal	4.3	8.2	91	0.5	0.9
Spain	27.4	60.7	122	0.8	1.7
Sweden	35.8	49.1	37	4.6	6.0
Switzerland	16.0	22.4	40	2.7	3.5
Turkey	14.8	27.2	84	0.5	0.7
United Kingdom	193.2	203.2	5	3.5	3.6
North America	1,343.9	1,890.6	41	6.3	8.0
Australia and New Zealand	44.1	69.5	58	3.2	4.1
OECD Europe	800.9	1,116.2	39	2.3	2.9
OECD Total	2,340.3	3,408.2	46	3.4	4.6

NOTES: a) Millions tons of oil equivalent.

b) Tons of oil equivalent.

Annex 16. TOTAL ANNUAL WATER WITHDRAWAL, SELECTED COUNTRIES, 1975

COUNTRY	TOTAL WITHDRAWAL (MILLION M^3)	TOTAL WITHDRAWAL PER CAPITA (M^3/CAPITA)
Canada[a]......................	27,600	1,230
USA	580,000	2,720
Japan[a]......................	77,920	707
Australia	16,900	1,242
New Zealand	1,040	336
Austria	2,620	347
Belgium	7,800	795
Denmark	1,210	239
France	24,200	458
Germany	33,216	537
Greece	4,270	472
Italy [b]	42,830	767
Netherlands[c]................	13,160	964
Norway [d]	2,380	602
Portugal	6,440	682
Sweden	7,700	939
Switzerland	690	112
Turkey[e]	11,760	293
United Kingdom [f]	13,640	278

NOTES:

a) 1974.

b) Components of total withdrawal are for 1967, 1970 and 1971.

c) 1976.

d) 1973.

e) 1970.

f) England and Wales only.

Annex 17. ANNUAL MEAN[a] LEVELS OF BIOLOGICAL OXYGEN DEMAND (BOD), SELECTED RIVERS, 1965-1975

COUNTRY	RIVERS	1965	1970	1975
USA[b]	Delaware	..	3. 2	2. 5
	Platte	..	14. 2	11. 9
Japan	Tama	6. 6	6. 8	7. 1
	Yodo[c]	3. 8	5. 2	2. 5
	Kiso[c]	4. 5	6. 0	1. 8
Austria	Drau[c]	2. 0	1. 8	1. 7
Belgium	Scheldt	..	4. 0	8. 2
France[d]	Seine	..	6. 7	4. 8
	Loire	..	6. 7	4. 4
	Rhone	..	2. 9	5. 5
Germany	Rhine	7. 2	7. 0	7. 9
Netherlands	Rhine	3. 9	3. 1	3. 2
Portugal[e]	Tagus	..	..	..
Switzerland[e]	Rhine	..	..	..
United Kingdom	Lee[f]	9. 5	8. 1	5. 2
	Wear	3. 7	5. 1	4. 5
	Irwell and Mersey[g]	22. 0	20. 2	9. 5

NOTES:

a) Measured in ppm, at mouth of river or national boundary (downstream).

b) Three years average figures for period 1968-1970 and 1974-1976, data for Platte river taken downstreams of Denver.

c) 1966 data in 1965 column.

d) 1971 data in 1970 column. 1976 data in 1975 column for the rivers Seine and Rhone.

e) Data provided in index form only.

f) 1967 data in 1965 column.

g) Data in 1965 column is an average figure for 1967/1968.

Annex 18.   DOMESTIC WASTE WATER TREATMENT[a], SELECTED COUNTRIES, 1965-1975

COUNTRY	PERCENTAGE OF NATIONAL POPULATION SERVED		
	1965	1970	1975
Canada	..	..	59[b]
USA[c]	55	66	77
Japan	7	16	23
New Zealand	69	77	80
Belgium	3	4	6
Denmark	..	56[d]	59
Finland	..	31	51
France	..	32	40
Germany[e]...............	51	64	80
Greece	..	..	11
Italy	..	12[f]	..
Netherlands	20	36	68[b]
Portugal	..	..	2
Sweden	62	66	81
Switzerland	..	..	60
United Kingdom	..	80	82

NOTES:

a)   At least primary (physical) treatment. Also includes some secondary (biological) and tertiary (chemical) treatments.

b)   Data refers to 1977.

c)   Data refers to 1962, 1968 and 1973.

d)   Data refers to 1972.

e)   Data refers to 1963, 1969 and 1977.

f)   Data refers to 1971.

COUNTRY	RIVER	1965	1970	1975
Canada[b]	Red and Nelson	..	..	..
Japan	Tama	2. 87	1. 96	3. 31
Austria[c]	Drau	1. 8	2. 0	2. 6
Belgium[d]	Maas	..	3. 9	9. 4
	Scheldt	..	3. 9	7. 75
France[e]	Seine	..	7. 5	18. 5
	Loire	..	7. 0	6. 4
	Rhone	..	3. 6	4. 2
Germany	Rhine	10. 1	11. 7	13. 8
Netherlands	Rhine	1. 7	2. 5	2. 8
Switzerland[b]	Rhine	..	..	..
United Kingdom	Lee[f]	9. 0	15. 0	19. 7
	Wear	1. 94	2. 13	3. 85
	Irwell and Mersey[g]	0. 6	1. 0	2. 3

NOTES:
a)   Measured in ppm, at mouth of river or national boundary (downstream).
b)   Data provided in index form only.
c)   1966 data in column 1965.
d)   1972 data for river Maas in column 1970,   1971 data for river Scheldt in column 1970.
e)   1971 data in column 1970,   1976 data for river Seine in column 1975.
f)   1967 data in column 1965.
g)   Data in column 1965 is an average figure for 1967/1968.

Annex 20. LAND USE IN OECD COUNTRIES, 1975

COUNTRY	ARABLE AND CROP LAND [a]		PERMANENT GRASSLAND		WOODED AREA		OTHER AREAS		TOTAL LAND = 100
	KM²	%	KM²	%	KM²	%	KM²	%	KM²
Canada	392,610	3.9	243,000	2.4	4,430,940	44.4	4,909,590	49.2	9,976,140
USA	1,910,000	20.3	2,440,000	26.0	2,888,450	30.8	2,125,000	22.6	9,363,450
Japan	55,720	14.9	2,420	0.6	250,430	67.2	63,740	17.1	372,310
Australia	450,490	5.8	4,556,480	59.2	937,450	12.1	1,742,440	22.6	7,686,860
New Zealand	9,890	3.6	129,600	48.2	63,200	23.5	65,980	24.5	268,670
Austria	16,080	19.3	21,810	26.2	32,500	39.1	12,600	15.1	82,990
Belgium	8,080	26.4	7,200	23.5	6,160	20.1	8,980	29.4	30,510
Denmark	26,600	61.7	2,770	6.4	4,810	11.1	8,890	20.6	43,070
Finland	26,410	7.8	1,600	0.4	186,970	55.4	122,050	36.2	337,030
France	189,220	34.4	134,050	24.4	146,080	26.6	79,740	14.5	549,090
Germany	75,380	30.5	52,440	21.0	71,620	28.8	48,010	19.4	248,590
Greece	39,200	29.7	49,300	37.3	26,400	20.0	17,040	12.9	131,940
Iceland	..	..	22,790	22.1	1,200	1.1	79,020	76.7	103,020
Ireland	12,480	17.7	35,990	51.2	2,950	4.1	18,860	26.8	70,280
Italy	123,130	40.8	52,040	17.2	63,060	20.9	63,030	20.9	301,260
Luxembourg	610	23.5	700	27.0	910	35.1	370	14.2	2,590
Netherlands	8,500	23.0	12,410	33.5	3,090	8.3	12,950	35.0	36,950
Norway	7,920	2.4	1,060	0.3	83,300	25.7	231,610	71.5	323,890
Portugal	36,700	41.2	5,300	5.9	25,000	28.1	21,940	24.6	88,940
Spain	208,330	41.2	72,260	14.3	149,440	29.6	74,710	14.8	504,740
Sweden	30,060	6.6	7,200	1.6	226,210	50.2	186,490	41.4	449,960
Switzerland	3,840	9.3	16,300	39.4	10,520	25.4	10,630	25.7	41,290
Turkey	276,570	35.4	261,350	33.4	201,700	25.8	40,960	5.2	780,580
United Kingdom	69,580	28.5	116,280	47.6	20,180	8.2	38,000	15.5	244,040
Yugoslavia	80,340	31.4	63,570	24.8	90,000	35.1	21,890	8.5	255,800
North America	2,302,610	11.9	2,683,000	13.8	7,319,390	37.8	7,134,590	36.9	19,339,590
Australia and New Zealand	460,380	5.8	4,686,080	58.9	1,000,650	12.6	1,808,420	22.7	7,955,530
OECD Europe	1,164,000	26.6	872,950	19.9	1,262,100	28.8	1,071,810	24.5	4,370,760
OECD Total	3,982,710	12.4	8,244,350	25.7	9,832,570	30.6	9,978,560	31.1	32,038,190

NOTES: a) "Arable and crop land" is defined as the sum of arable area and of land under permanent crop. "other areas" include built up land, desert, tundras, muskeg, ice, dunes, mountains, inland waters.

Percentages accross columns do not add up exactly to 100% due to rounding procedures.

COUNTRY	AREA OF HABITABLE LAND		AREA OF BUILT UP LAND	
	MID 1970's KM^2	AS PERCENTAGE IN TOTAL LAND %	MID 1970's KM^2	AS PERCENTAGE IN TOTAL LAND %
Canada	2,194,750[b]	22[b]	6,800[c]	0.2[c]
USA	4,842,080	52	390,410	4.2
Japan	81,640	22	20,000	5.3
Australia	5,642,580[d]	73	7,490	0.1
New Zealand	141,890[e]	53	2,400	0.9
Austria	38,890[e]	47	1,000[f]	1.2[f]
Belgium	23,410	77	8,130	26.6
Denmark	33,120[e]	77	4,640	10.7
Finland	36,010[e]	10	8,000	2.4
France	380,850	69	29,250	5.3
Germany	154,060	62	23,290	9.4
Greece[g]	95,300[e]	72	6,800	5.1
Iceland	..	..	..	..
Ireland	49,880[e]	71	1,410	2.0
Italy	208,730[h]	69	..	..
Luxembourg	..	..	..	..
Netherlands	26,290	71	3,800	9.2
Norway	15,980[e]	5	7,000	2.1
Portugal	47,290[e]	53	5,290	5.9
Spain	335,900	67	18,770	3.7
Sweden	70,280	16	11,500	2.5
Switzerland	21,940[e]	53	1,800	4.2
Turkey	544,190	70	5,700	0.7
United Kingdom	221,350	91	29,230	11.9

NOTES:
a)   Habitable area is defined here as the sum total of:
   i) utilized agricultural area (permanent grassland and arable land - including family garden and fallow land);
   ii) non-utilized agricultural area (including waste land and moors but excluding forests); and
   iii) built up area (the land taken up by settlements, industry and transport).
   Uninhabitable area is therefore defined as the sum total of forest land, unusable land (including deserts, dunes and mountains), and interior waters.
   Forest land is not habitable in many countries for climatic reasons or in mountainous areas. Though for some countries important parts of forest land may be suitable for habitation (flat areas - valleys - hills ...). The definition of habitable land may therefore be misleading for some countries.
b)   Different definition. Therefore comparison should be avoided.
c)   Urban settlements over 25,000 people only.
d)   Does not include built up land and unused agricultural areas.
e)   Does not include unused agricultural areas.
f)   Land covered by buildings only.
g)   1961.
h)   Does not include built up land.

Annex 22. CONSUMPTION OF AGRICULTURAL LAND FOR BUILT UP USES, SELECTED COUNTRIES, 1960-1970

COUNTRY	PERCENTAGE OF AGRICULTURAL LAND LOST FOR BUILT UP USES[a] 1960-1970
USA	0.8
Japan	7.3
New Zealand[b]	0.5
Austria	1.8
Belgium[c]	12.3
Denmark	3.0
Finland[d]	2.8
France	1.8
Germany	2.5
Netherlands	4.3
Norway	1.5
Sweden	3.3
Turkey	0.4
United Kingdom	1.8

NOTES:

a) OECD calculations based on estimates of the extension of land taken up by built up uses. Due to these assumptions, and to differences in dates and definitions, these data are only rough estimates and mainly indicate the scale of the process. For detail see: OECD (1976) "Land use policy and agriculture", Paris.

b) Excludes communication systems.

c) Includes unusable land and non-navigable internal waterways, except ponds.

d) Does not include all built up areas.

Annex 23. TOTAL EMISSIONS[a] OF MAJOR AIR POLLUTANTS, SELECTED COUNTRIES, 1965-1975

COUNTRY	PARTICULATES		SO$_2$		NO$_x$		CO		HC	
	1965	1975	1965	1975	1965	1975	1965	1975	1965	1975
Canada[b]	..	100.6	..	85.6	..	153.0	..	81.3	..	88.6
USA	..	63.7	..	88.3	..	108.8	..	86.1	..	88.2
Japan	..	..	62.0	52.0	48.0	107.9	..	..	..	..
Finland	85.7	108.0	79.8	105.7	74.4	116.2	68.4	118.4	..	..
France[c]	81.6	49.4	73.8	147.0	65.3	132.0	75.0	116.6	76.0	93.4
Germany	202.8	47.6	96.9	85.1	82.5	114.0	..	..	79.4	98.4
Italy[d]	70.0	..	61.7	..	63.8	112.9	67.9	..	69.6	79.5
Netherlands	136.0	73.3	130.5	58.4	82.8	105.6	96.0	99.2	101.7	100.9
Norway	..	..	..	..	..	93.6	..	..	..	123.8
Portugal[e]	..	47.6	..	173.9	..	141.0	..	165.0	..	169.0
Spain[f]	60.2	126.2	62.1	151.8	54.5	135.7	..	..	..	..
Sweden	..	150.0	86.0	79.0	67.0	170.0	..	150.0	..	252.0
Switzerland[g]	..	..	..	..	..	166.0	..	124.0	..	116.0
United Kingdom[h]	159.7	54.2	98.2	86.3	..	93.3	..	104.2	..	102.9

NOTES:

a) Measured in tons, base 100 in 1970.
b) Data refers to 1976 for NO$_x$ and to 1974 for other emissions in 1975 columns.
c) Stationary sources only for particulates, mobile sources only for CO and HC.
d) Data refers to 1966, 1971, 1974 for SO$_x$, and 1966, 1971 and 1972 for NO$_x$ and HC.
e) From liquid fuel combustion only.
f) Stationary sources only from industry and energy related activities.
g) Mobile sources only.
h) Smoke from coal combustion only for particulates, base 100 in 1969 for CO and HC.

Annex 24. EMISSIONS OF MAJOR AIR POLLUTANTS, SELECTED COUNTRIES, 1975 [a]

COUNTRY	EMISSION PER CAPITA kg/capita					EMISSION PER UNIT OF GDP tns/10⁶ US$					EMISSION PER UNIT OF ENERGY CONSUMED tns/10³ TOE				
	PART.	SO₂	NOₓ	CO	HC	SO₂	NOₓ	CO	HC	PART.	PART.	SO₂	NOₓ	CO	HC
Canada [b]	96	249	84	620	101	35	12	87	14	13	11	28	9.4	69	11
USA	67	120	103	402	122	17	14.7	56	17	9.5	8.5	15	13	51	15
Japan	..	25	20	..	..	5.6	4.7	..	..	..	..	8.3	6.9	..	..
Australia [c]	189	107	67	459	113	16	10	68	17	28	39	22	14	96	24
Austria [b]	7	45	15	129	6	8.8	3	25.9	1.2	1.4	2.3	15	3	42	2
Denmark [b,d]	..	17	8.9	52	6.5	2.4	1.3	7.5	0.9	..	..	4.7	2.5	15	1.8
Finland	56	116	53	95	..	21	9.6	17	..	10.3	12	25	11	20	..
France [e,d]	11	53	25	132	8.1	8.3	3.8	20.8	1.3	1.8	3.6	17	7.7	42	25
Germany	8	59	31	..	30	8.6	4.6	..	4.4	1.2	2.1	15	7.9	..	7.7
Greece [f]	30	17	..	12	..	7.3	..	5.1	..	13	23	13	..	9	..
Italy [l,g]	..	47	17	..	22	15.3	5.6	..	7	..	..	21	7.5	..	9.5
Netherlands	14.5	31	30	121	30	5.2	5.0	20	5.0	2.4	3.3	7.2	7.0	28	69
Norway [h]	..	30	26	..	40	4.3	3.6	..	5.7	..	..	6.4	5.4	..	8.4
Portugal [h]	4	37	21	82	8.8	12	6.8	27	5.7	1.2	2.4	24	14	54	10.2
Spain [i]	36	46	6.3	..	..	16	2.2	..	..	13	21.4	27	3.7	..	..
Sweden	21	84	38	171	52	10	4.5	20	6.2	2.5	3.5	14	6.3	28.5	8.6
Switzerland [g,j]	..	22	2.3	22	2.2	2.6	0.3	2.6	0.3	..	..	6.7	0.7	6.4	0.6
Turkey [g]	..	12	..	..	..	13.8	..	..	..	..	..	16	..	..	..
United Kingdom [k]	7	94	30	138	20	23.2	7.4	34	4.9	1.7	4.6	26	8.3	38	55

NOTES:

a) Emission data are for 1975; unless otherwise stated. The population, gross domestic product and energy consumption data refer to 1975. Several ratios are therefore not strictly comparable.

b) 1974, NOₓ is for 1976 in Canada.

c) 1971.

d) Mobile sources only for CO and HC.

e) Stationary sources only for particulates.

f) 1973, mobile sources only for CO.

g) Figures refer to 1974 and fuel combustion in stationary sources only for SO₂.

h) Liquid fuel combustion and stationary sources only for HC and CO.

i) Stationary sources only from industry and energy related activities.

j) Mobile sources only for NOₓ, CO and HC.

k) Smoke from coal combustion only for particulates.

l) 1972.

Annex 25.   EMISSIONS OF SULPHUR DIOXIDE (SO$_2$) AND
NITROGEN OXIDES (NO$_x$) PER UNIT OF ENERGY CONSUMED,
SELECTED COUNTRIES, 1965-1975

COUNTRY	SO$_2$ tons/1,000 TOE			NO$_x$ tons/1,000 TOE		
	1965	1970	1975	1965	1970	1975
Canada	..	42	28[a]	..	7.9	9.4[b]
USA	..	18.5	15	..	13	13
Japan	21.6	18.5	8.3	6.7	7.5	6.9
Finland	28	27	25	10.9	11	11.2
France	12	12.6	17	5.5	6.5	7.7
Germany	22.6	18.2	15	..	7.2	7.9
Netherlands	30	14.8	7.2	10.2	7.9	7
Norway	..	..	6.4	..	6.3	5.4
Sweden	19.4	18.4	14	..	4.1	6.3
United Kingdom	31	29	26	6.9[c]	6.7[d]	6.7

NOTES:
a) 1974.
b) 1976.
c) 1966.
d) 1969.

Annex 26. POPULATION EXPOSED[a] TO OUTDOOR CONCENTRATIONS OF AIR POLLUTION IN EXCESS OF SPECIFIED LEVELS[b], SELECTED COUNTRIES, 1970–1975

COUNTRY	NATIONAL POPULATION 1970 (MILLION INHABITANTS)	STUDIED POPULATION (A)		PERCENTAGE OF STUDIED POPULATION EXPOSED			
		MILLION INHABITANTS	% OF TOTAL POPULATION	SO₂ (B)		PARTICULATES (B)	
				1970	1975	1970	1975
Canada	22.5[c]	12.7	56	100	54	99	98
USA	204.9	165	80.5	..	..	45	28
Japan	103.4	103.4	100	46	..	..	25.4
Belgium	9.6	9.6	100	26.5	25.4	26.5	84
France	52.6[d]	23.3	44.3	..	77	..	..
Norway	3.8	3.8	100	3	1.5	0.2	0.09
United Kingdom[g],[e]	56.0	7.3[f]	13	66	55	26	1.6
United Kingdom[g],[f]		4.3	8	58	25		

NOTES:

a) The percentage of the population exposed (columns B) is related to a studied population (column A) which may not be the total population of the country; it concerns the exposure to both SO₂ and particulates. This table shows that the informations remain insufficient on such an important indicator.

b) The air quality levels and the methods of measurements are those specified by the Member countries. Because of differences, any comparison between countries should be avoided.

Canada: SO₂: 60 μg/m³. Part.: 70 μg/m³.

USA: Part.: 15 μg/m³.

Japan: SO₂: 104 μg/m³.

Belgium: Population exposed considered as being the total population of the following towns: Bruxels, Gand, Charleroi, Antwerpen and Liege.

Norway: SO₂: 2% of observation in excess of 200 μg/m³.

UK: SO₂: 80 μg/m³ annual average. Part.: 60 μg/m³ smoke annual average.

Threshold used for other countries:

SO₂: 60 μg/m³ (annual average) and/or 2% of the observations being above 200 μg/m³ (24 hourly value).

Part.: 40 μg/m³ (annual average) and/or 2% of the observations being above 120 μg/m³ (24 hourly value).

c) Population is for 1974; data on exposure are for 1970 and 1974.

d) Population is for 1975; the studied population relates to 18 urban areas over 100,000 inhabitants.

e) Greater London population; population figure is for 1973.

f) Greater Manchester and Merseyside population.

g) 1970 column (except for population) refers to 1972/3 and the 1975 column refers to 1975/6.

Annex 27. FISHING AND HUNTING LICENSES, SELECTED COUNTRIES, 1975

COUNTRY	NUMBER OF FISHING LICENSES 1,000	NUMBER OF HUNTING LICENSES 1,000	PERCENTAGE OF NATIONAL POPULATION HOLDING FISH- ING LICENSES	PERCENTAGE OF NATIONAL POPULATION HOLDING HUNT- ING LICENSES
Canada	..	2,456	..	11.0
United States ...	27,517	16,598	12.9	7.8
Japan	..	517[a]	..	0.4
Austria[b]	..	93	..	1.2
Belgium	200	29	2.0	0.3
Finland	456	231	9.6	4.9
France	2,585	2,209	4.9	4.1
Germany[c]	..	221	..	0.4
Netherlands	895	38	6.5	0.3
Norway	272	118[d]	6.8	2.9
Portugal	69	..	0.7	..
Sweden	1,000 to 1,500	220	12 to 18	2.6
Switzerland	150 to 200	..	2.5 to 3	..
Turkey	90	130[e]	0.2	0.3
United Kingdom .	576[f]	..	1.0	..

NOTES:
a) Mammals only. Excludes birds.
b) 1976.
c) 1965.
d) Big game only.
e) Birds only.
f) Trout fishing only.

Annex 28. PROTECTED NATURAL AREAS AND WILDLIFE REFUGES, SELECTED COUNTRIES, 1970-1975

COUNTRY	PROTECTED NATURAL AREAS AND WILDLIFE REFUGES Km2		PERCENT OF COUNTRY IN PROTECTED NATURAL AREAS AND WILDLIFE REFUGES	
	1970	1975	1970	1975
Canada[a]	..	115,546	..	1.2
USA[b]	267,308	283,324	3.0	3.1
Japan	18,172	26,740	4.9	7.2
Australia	53,940	88,300	0.7	1.1
New Zealand[c]	6,231	6,581	2.3	2.4
Belgium	108	179	0.35	0.6
Finland[d]	925	2,730	0.27	0.81
France[e]	1,916	3,064	0.35	0.56
Germany[d]	2,878	8,400	1.2	2.6
Greece[f]	2,501	6,400	1.9	4.9
Netherlands	682	947	1.8	2.6
Norway[g]	25	156	0.008	0.048
Spain[h]	..	15,000	..	3.0
Sweden[d]	613	2,658	0.14	0.59
United Kingdom	910	..	0.4	..

NOTES: Comparisons between countries should be avoided due to difference in definitions of protected areas and the extent of protection.

a) Includes wildlife sanctuaries and national wildlife areas.

b) Includes Federal protected areas - National Wildlife Refuges, Natural Areas in National Parks, and National Wilderness Preservation System. Excludes state and private wildlife refuges.

c) Includes reserves for preservation of flora and fauna and wilderness preservation areas.

d) Includes all protected areas outside of National and Regional Parks - i.e., wildlife refuges, countryside and coastline preservation, wilderness preservation, and historical and cultural sites.

e) Includes inland wildlife refuges and central area of national parks.

f) These are totally protected areas and can be considered as national and regional parks as well as wildlife refuges and wilderness preservation areas.

g) Includes nature reserves.

h) Game reserves.

Annex 29. ENVIRONMENTAL CONTAMINANTS IN WILDLIFE SAMPLES, OECD COUNTRIES, 1972-1975

COUNTRY	SAMPLING ENVIRONMENT	TRENDS[a] IN CONCENTRATION IN 1972-1975		
		DDE	PCBs	MERCURY
Canada	marine	−	−	..
	marine	−	o	..
	freshwater	−	−	o
	terrestrial	o	..	o
	terrestrial	−	..	..
	terrestrial	o	..	..
USA	marine	+	+	..
	freshwater	−	−	..
	terrestrial	o	+	..
	terrestrial	o	+	..
Japan	marine	−	−	o
	freshwater	..	o	−
	freshwater	..	o	−
	terrestrial	..	−	−
	terrestrial	o	o	−
Austria	freshwater	..	−	+
	freshwater	..	+	+
Belgium	marine	−	o	−
	marine	..	..	−
	freshwater	..	..	−
Finland	marine	−	o	..
	marine	−	−	..
	freshwater	−	−	o
	freshwater	−	o	−
	terrestrial	o	o	..
France	marine	..	..	+
	marine	..	..	o
	freshwater	+	..	(+)(−) [b]
	freshwater	..	..	−
	terrestrial	−	−	o
	terrestrial	+	o	..
Netherlands	marine	−	−	−
	freshwater	o	o	o
	freshwater	o	o	−
Norway	marine	−	−	+
	marine	−	−	o
	freshwater	..	o	..
	freshwater	..	..	+
Portugal	marine	o	+	..
	freshwater	−	..	..
	freshwater	o	o	..
Sweden	marine	−	o	−
	marine	−	o	o
	freshwater	o	−	−
	freshwater	o	o	−
	terrestrial	−	−	−
	terrestrial	+	..	−
	terrestrial	..	o	−
Switzerland	freshwater	−	−	o
	terrestrial	o	o	..
	terrestrial	+	o	+
United Kingdom	marine	−	o	+
	marine	−	−	..
	marine	−	o	+
	freshwater	−	o	..
	freshwater	o	+	..
	terrestrial	o	..	..

TRENDS: + increase;   − decrease;   o no trends;   .. no trend studied.
NOTES:
a.   Trends have been studied over 2, 3 or 4 years according to the different sampling sites and the contaminants analysed.
b.   Opposite trends for different types of fishes at some sampling site.

Annex 30.   IMPORTANCE ATTACHED TO VARIOUS ISSUES, EEC COUNTRIES, 1976

ISSUES	EEC[a]	BELGIUM	DENMARK	FRANCE	GERMANY	IRELAND	ITALY	LUXEMBOURG	NETHERLANDS	UNITED KINGDOM
Fight unemployment	2.71	2.72	2.76	2.75	2.66	2.85	..	2.47	2.74	2.63
Fight inflation	2.68	2.69	2.58	2.68	2.63	2.87	2.75	2.64	2.46	2.70
Protect nature and control pollution	2.49	2.53	2.70	2.73	2.36	2.38	2.46	2.57	2.58	2.41
Protect consumers	2.43	2.50	2.57	2.51	2.36	2.56	2.56	2.17	2.41	2.31
Build enough housing	2.30	2.16	2.02	2.30	1.91	2.69	2.60	2.33	2.25	2.49
Adapt schooling to needs of modern man	2.14	2.29	1.97	2.29	2.30	2.42	2.21	2.35	2.20	2.04
Reduce income differentials	2.06	2.17	2.13	2.33	1.87	2.19	2.45	2.31	2.11	1.57
Protect our country from super-powers	1.95	1.95	2.14	2.22	1.91	1.74	2.06	2.04	1.90	2.12
Reduce regional differentials	1.90	1.86	2.11	2.00	1.57	2.19	2.29	2.15	1.98	1.84
Control multi-national corporations	1.90	2.05	2.36	2.09	1.84	2.00	2.08	2.20	1.86	1.57
Reinforce our military power	1.51	0.97	1.53	1.51	1.43	1.57	1.24	1.25	1.45	1.98
Increase regional autonomy	1.48	1.61	1.89	1.75	1.30	1.56	1.66	1.87	1.46	1.19

NOTES: This table concerns an opinion poll made in the 9 countries of the European Communities.

The sample size was 8,627 people aged over 15 years. Respondents were asked to say wether they thought these issues were:

Very important   (graded 3)
Important   (graded 2)
Not very important   (graded 1)
Or Not important at all   (graded 0)

a)   Weighted average.

SOURCE: Euro-Baromètre N° 5, July 1976.

175

Annex 31. PERCEPTION OF THE SERIOUSNESS OF ENVIRONMENTAL PROBLEMS, BY URBAN RESIDENTS IN JAPAN AND UNITED STATES, 1974

ENVIRONMENTAL PROBLEM	JAPAN	UNITED STATES
- is not a serious problem	3.6	3.3
- is a matter of specific abuses rather than a basic threat to our society	9.1	24.2
- is a serious long-range threat .	21.8	47.3
- threatens disaster in the near future or now	34.6	20.9
- at present, already critically threatening	30.9	not asked
- don't know, cannot decide	not asked	3.3
Total	100.0	100.0

NOTE: The survey differentiated between "urban" and "rural" respondents, but showed that their answers did not differ very much.

SOURCE: Yoshii, H., International Comparative Beliefs Study: Perceptions of Environmental Quality, Tokyo, Institute for Future Technology, March 1976, p. 12.

LIST OF THE MEMBERS OF THE GROUP OF EXPERTS ON THE STATE OF THE ENVIRONMENT

Australia

Mr. J. BELL
Mr. D. MacRAE

Austria

Mr. E. MUSYL

Belgium

Mr. J. BOUQUIAUX
Miss M. ROBERT

Canada

Mr. T. DE FAYER
Mr. A. FRIEND
Mr. P. HEINBECKER

Finland

Mr. A. LAIHONEN
Mr. T. LEPPO

France

Mr. P. CORNIERE
Mr. R. CRUON
Mr. Y. RECHNER

Germany

Mr. V. HASSEMER
Mr. V. HERING
Mr. M. UPPENBRINK

Greece

Mr. P. LAGOS
Mr. J. TZITZIS

Japan

Mr. H. HAMANAKA
Mr. M. SAKURAI

Netherlands

Mr. R. HUETING
Mr. J. KARRES
Mr. A. DE KORT

Norway

Mr. E. BORSET
Mr. E. HOFFMANN

Sweden

Mr. B. MALMAS
Mrs. I. PALMLUND
Mrs. U. SWAREN

Turkey

Mrs. F. EKE
Mr. S. ULLIG

United Kingdom

Mr. P. MacCORMACK

Yugoslavia

Mrs. S. BOROVNICA

OECD Secretariat

Mr. C. AVEROUS

OECD SALES AGENTS
DÉPOSITAIRES DES PUBLICATIONS DE L'OCDE

ARGENTINA – ARGENTINE
Carlos Hirsch S.R.L., Florida 165,
BUENOS-AIRES, Tel. 33-1787-2391 Y 30-7122

AUSTRALIA – AUSTRALIE
Australia & New Zealand Book Company Pty Ltd.,
23 Cross Street, (P.O.B. 459)
BROOKVALE NSW 2100 Tel. 938-2244

AUSTRIA – AUTRICHE
Gerold and Co., Graben 31, WIEN 1. Tel. 52.22.35

BELGIUM – BELGIQUE
LCLS
44 rue Otlet, B1070 BRUXELLES .Tel. 02-521 28 13

BRAZIL – BRÉSIL
Mestre Jou S.A., Rua Guaipá 518,
Caixa Postal 24090, 05089 SAO PAULO 10. Tel. 261-1920
Rua Senador Dantas 19 s/205-6, RIO DE JANEIRO GB.
Tel. 232-07. 32

CANADA
Renouf Publishing Company Limited,
2182 St. Catherine Street West,
MONTREAL, Quebec H3H 1M7 Tel. (514) 937-3519

DENMARK – DANEMARK
Munksgaards Boghandel,
Nørregade 6, 1165 KØBENHAVN K. Tel. (01) 12 85 70

FINLAND – FINLANDE
Akateeminen Kirjakauppa
Keskuskatu 1, 00100 HELSINKI 10. Tel. 625.901

FRANCE
Bureau des Publications de l'OCDE,
2 rue André-Pascal, 75775 PARIS CEDEX 16. Tel. (1) 524.81.67
Principal correspondant :
13602 AIX-EN-PROVENCE : Librairie de l'Université.
Tel. 26.18.08

GERMANY – ALLEMAGNE
Alexander Horn,
D - 6200 WIESBADEN, Spiegelgasse 9
Tel. (6121) 37-42-12

GREECE – GRÈCE
Librairie Kauffmann, 28 rue du Stade,
ATHÈNES 132. Tel. 322.21.60

HONG-KONG
Government Information Services,
Sales and Publications Office, Beaconsfield House, 1st floor,
Queen's Road, Central. Tel. H-233191

ICELAND – ISLANDE
Snaebjörn Jönsson and Co., h.f.,
Hafnarstraeti 4 and 9, P.O.B. 1131, REYKJAVIK.
Tel. 13133/14281/11936

INDIA – INDE
Oxford Book and Stationery Co.:
NEW DELHI, Scindia House. Tel. 45896
CALCUTTA. 17 Park Street. Tel. 240832

ITALY – ITALIE
Libreria Commissionaria Sansoni:
Via Lamarmora 45, 50121 FIRENZE. Tel. 579751
Via Bartolini 29, 20155 MILANO. Tel. 365083
Sub-depositari:
Editrice e Libreria Herder,
Piazza Montecitorio 120, 00 186 ROMA. Tel. 674628
Libreria Hoepli, Via Hoepli 5, 20121 MILANO. Tel. 865446
Libreria Lattes, Via Garibaldi 3, 10122 TORINO. Tel. 519274
La diffusione delle edizioni OCSE è inoltre assicurata dalle migliori
librerie nelle città più importanti.

JAPAN – JAPON
OECD Publications and Information Center
Akasaka Park Building, 2-3-4 Akasaka, Minato-ku,
TOKYO 107. Tel. 586-2016

KOREA - CORÉE
Pan Korea Book Corporation,
P.O.Box n° 101 Kwangwhamun, SÉOUL. Tel. 72-7369

LEBANON – LIBAN
Documenta Scientifica/Redico,
Edison Building, Bliss Street, P.O.Box 5641, BEIRUT.
Tel. 354429–344425

MEXICO & CENTRAL AMERICA
Centro de Publicaciones de Organismos Internacionales S.A.,
Alfonso Herrera N° 72, 1er Piso,
Apdo. Postal 42-051, MEXICO 4 D.F.

THE NETHERLANDS – PAYS-BAS
Staatsuitgeverij
Chr. Plantijnstraat
'S-GRAVENHAGE. Tel. 070-814511
Voor bestellingen: Tel. 070-624551

NEW ZEALAND – NOUVELLE-ZÉLANDE
The Publications Manager,
Government Printing Office,
WELLINGTON: Mulgrave Street (Private Bag),
World Trade Centre, Cubacade, Cuba Street,
Rutherford House, Lambton Quay, Tel. 737-320
AUCKLAND: Rutland Street (P.O.Box 5344), Tel. 32.919
CHRISTCHURCH: 130 Oxford Tce (Private Bag), Tel. 50.331
HAMILTON: Barton Street (P.O.Box 857), Tel. 80.103
DUNEDIN: T & G Building, Princes Street (P.O.Box 1104),
Tel. 78.294

NORWAY – NORVÈGE
J.G. TANUM A/S,
P.O. Box 1177 Sentrum, OSLO 1

PAKISTAN
Mirza Book Agency, 65 Shahrah Quaid-E-Azam, LAHORE 3.
Tel. 66839

PORTUGAL
Livraria Portugal, Rua do Carmo 70-74,
1117 LISBOA CODEX.
Tel. 360582/3

SPAIN – ESPAGNE
Mundi-Prensa Libros, S.A.
Castelló 37, Apartado 1223, MADRID-1. Tel. 275.46.55
Libreria Bastinos, Pelayo, 52, BARCELONA 1. Tel. 222.06.00

SWEDEN – SUÈDE
AB CE Fritzes Kungl Hovbokhandel,
Box 16 356, S 103 27 STH, Regeringsgatan 12,
DS STOCKHOLM. Tel. 08/23 89 00

SWITZERLAND – SUISSE
Librairie Payot, 6 rue Grenus, 1211 GENÈVE 11. Tel. 022-31.89.50

TAIWAN – FORMOSE
National Book Company,
84-5 Sing Sung Rd., Sec. 3, TAIPEI 107. Tel. 321.0698

UNITED KINGDOM – ROYAUME-UNI
H.M. Stationery Office, P.O.B. 569,
LONDON SEI 9 NH. Tel. 01-928-6977, Ext. 410 or
49 High Holborn, LONDON WC1V 6 HB (personal callers)
Branches at: EDINBURGH, BIRMINGHAM, BRISTOL,
MANCHESTER, CARDIFF, BELFAST.

UNITED STATES OF AMERICA
OECD Publications and Information Center, Suite 1207,
1750 Pennsylvania Ave., N.W. WASHINGTON. D.C.20006.
Iel. (202)724-1857

VENEZUELA
Libreria del Este, Avda. F. Miranda 52, Edificio Galipán,
CARACAS 106. Tel. 32 23 01/33 26 04/33 24 73

YUGOSLAVIA – YOUGOSLAVIE
Jugoslovenska Knjiga, Terazije 27, P.O.B. 36, BEOGRAD.
Tel. 621-992

Les commandes provenant de pays où l'OCDE n'a pas encore désigné de dépositaire peuvent être adressées à :
OCDE, Bureau des Publications, 2 rue André-Pascal, 75775 PARIS CEDEX 16.
Orders and inquiries from countries where sales agents have not yet been appointed may be sent to:
OECD, Publications Office, 2 rue André-Pascal, 75775 PARIS CEDEX 16.

OECD PUBLICATIONS, 2 rue André-Pascal, 75775 Paris Cedex 16 - No. 41 217 1979
PRINTED IN FRANCE
(97 79 06 1) ISBN 92-64-11946-9

SOCIAL SCIENCE LIBRARY

Manor Road Building
Manor Road
Oxford OX1 3UQ
Tel: (2)71093 (enquiries and renewals)
http://www.ssl.ox.ac.uk

This is a NORMAL LOAN item.

We will email you a reminder before this item is due.

Please see http://www.ssl.ox.ac.uk/lending.html
for details on:

- loan policies; these are also displayed on the notice boards and in our library guide.

- how to check when your books are due back.

- how to renew your books, including information on the maximum number of renewals. Items may be renewed if not reserved by another reader. Items must be renewed before the library closes on the due date.

- level of fines; fines are charged on overdue books.

Please note that this item may be recalled during Term.

302534570T